Cracking the Code of Education Reform

Gabriella and Francesca

*"If you're ever alone, then your heart will know, it can reach to mine,
I'll be at your side."*

(Delonge, T., 2010)

I piccoli cugini

Luca, Fabio, Flavio, Giulia, Claudia, Giorgia

Cracking the Code of Education Reform

Creative Compliance and Ethical Leadership

Christopher H. Tienken

Foreword by Joshua Starr,
CEO of PDK International

FOR INFORMATION:

Corwin

A SAGE Company

2455 Teller Road

Thousand Oaks, California 91320

(800) 233-9936

www.corwin.com

SAGE Publications Ltd.

1 Oliver's Yard

55 City Road

London EC1Y 1SP

United Kingdom

SAGE Publications India Pvt. Ltd.

B 1/I 1 Mohan Cooperative Industrial Area

Mathura Road, New Delhi 110 044

India

SAGE Publications Asia-Pacific Pte. Ltd.

18 Cross Street #10-10/11/12

China Square Central

Singapore 048423

Publisher: Arnis Burvikovs

Development Editor: Desirée A. Bartlett

Senior Editorial Assistant: Eliza Erickson

Production Editor: Astha Jaiswal

Copy Editor: Michelle Ponce

Typesetter: C&M Digitals (P) Ltd.

Proofreader: Theresa Kay

Indexer: Celia McCoy

Cover Designer: Candice Harman

Graphic Designer: Mackenzie Lowry

Marketing Manager: Sharon Pendergast

Printed in the United States of America

ISBN 978-1-5443-6821-4

This book is printed on acid-free paper.

Certified Chain of Custody
Promoting Sustainable Forestry
www.sfiprogram.org
SFI-01268

SFI label applies to text stock

19 20 21 22 23 10 9 8 7 6 5 4 3 2 1

DISCLAIMER: This book may direct you to access third-party content via web links, QR codes, or other scannable technologies, which are provided for your reference by the author(s). Corwin makes no guarantee that such third-party content will be available for your use and encourages you to review the terms and conditions of such third-party content. Corwin takes no responsibility and assumes no liability for your use of any third-party content, nor does Corwin approve, sponsor, endorse, verify, or certify such third-party content.

Contents

Part II   Reform Case Studies   55

Part III   Promising Practices   107

Foreword

When I was superintendent of Stamford, CT, we were part of a nation-wide grant from the GE foundation to increase student achievement, especially in STEM-related areas. As part of this initiative, I got to know some GE executives and was fortunate to learn a little bit about how they lead change. An executive said to me once that he didn't want compliance, he wanted commitment. At GE they were all about leadership, culture, and processes. Simply complying with directives may meet an immediate need, but it didn't lead to long-term success. If the culture and decision-making processes are strong and unified, then leaders don't need to micromanage and direct everything an employee does.

At the time, we were in the midst of a major overhaul of systems and structures to support equity and higher levels of achievement throughout the Stamford public schools. I was a subscriber to the "fidelity of implementation" theory of action grounded in the idea that teachers and principals needed to follow the playbook to the letter, and good results would follow. New curriculum and materials, professional learning, common assessments, and new accountability measures were wrapped up in a comprehensive package that was clearly laid out for all to follow. I was organizing around compliance, not commitment. As Mike Tyson famously said, "everyone has a plan until they get punched in the mouth." I didn't get punched in the mouth when I was superintendent (at least not literally), but the comprehensive plan only got us so far. It wasn't until we loosened up the reins a little and allowed school leaders to operate within our framework yet act according to their own contexts that we saw increased improvement.

Given the last generation of top-down reforms that have been perpetuated on schools by distant policymakers and supported by funders, the marketplace, and the media, it's remarkable that so many school leaders continue to follow district directives rather than resist policies that don't always serve students well. Chris Tienken not only calls into question the legitimacy of many of the changes that have been enacted on public schools during the last generation of reform, but he provides useful tools and frameworks for school leaders to consider the value of those reforms to their schools. Fidelity has been the bailiwick of school improvement efforts for 20 years, yet we haven't seen the improvement that we'd like. Tienken suggests that school leaders consider the ethics of those efforts and then resist if necessary, by using specific strategies.

If I were still a superintendent, Tienken's ideas would make me nervous. As an educator and a father, it's exactly what I think we need. In fact, system leaders should be nervous about the ethics and impact of the reforms they push from on high. They should listen to the resisters, too, as their reasons for doing so can contain truths that leaders need to be aware of. Resistance may not be rejection of the intent of the underlying reform; there may be, in fact, shared interests. However, the impact that the execution of that interest may have on teachers, families, and students could have damaging—albeit unintended—consequences. Tienken gives leaders a decision-making framework and strategies for exercising ethical resistance.

The job of an educator has become increasingly complex. Funding has decreased while standards have risen. More attention is being paid to the social and emotional needs of students, yet high academic standards for all, as measured by standardized tests, is still the mountain we're trying to climb. Students are being encouraged to find their passions and discover pathways to successful college and career options. More technology is being developed, personalization has become a mantra for many, and perhaps most importantly, educators have begun to realize that race matters, and a mostly white teaching force has to learn how to engage with, value, and respect students from different backgrounds. Educators, especially leaders, have to make decisions in the midst of this complexity. Moreover, the federal government has backed off the aggressive overreach of the Bush and Obama administrations, which has left many state departments in a nebulous state. Districts can take advantage of this by pushing reforms that comport with their local context. But school leaders must determine whether a new initiative, policy, or program will benefit or harm their students. Chris Tienken has given them very specific ways to make those decisions.

Joshua Starr, EdD
Chief Executive Officer, PDK International

Acknowledgments

Although only my name appears as the author, I am indebted to the inspiration and collaboration provided by others. I would be incredibly naïve to think I could have written this alone. I acknowledge gratefully the support from my Corwin editors, Arnis Burvikovs, Desirée Bartlett, and Eliza Erickson. Their expert feedback and encouragement were delivered in ways that made the completion of this work possible. A special thanks to the anonymous Corwin reviewers for their incredibly supportive and instructive comments. They provided the valuable feedback I needed from the field to make this book useful to others.

I continue to think of my academic mentor, Dr. Charles Achilles, who dedicated his career to improving education for all children. The profession lost a great resource on February 8, 2013. The work of Drs. Daniel and Laurel Tanner on the Curriculum Paradigm continues to influence my thinking on education.

I thank Dr. Daniel Gutmore for his critique and thoughtful feedback on the first part of the book. He helped me clarify ideas and messages within the book and provided input and examples for successful creative compliance strategies. Thanks to Anthony Colella for the ongoing cognitive coaching and support.

This book calls for school leaders to take action, and I am inspired by an intrepid group of leaders who take action daily to improve the lives of children. They devoted time to read draft chapters or provide targeted feedback and ideas or help clarify my thinking: Drs. Patrick Michel, Clifford Burns, Dario Sforza, and Jennifer Luff, Mr. Kenyon Kummings, and Mrs. Jamie Moscony. Special thanks to Dr. Ralph Ferrie, a master of creative compliance and getting great things done for kids. Thanks to Yong Zhao for suggesting Corwin.

Gratitude to Mr. Joe Lisi for his ongoing support, inspiration, encouragement, and being a role model for what it means to be resilient. Thanks to Pappy who claims he can still hang a Woolwich tuxedo. God bless Lucille.

Grazie mille: Sicilia bedda, San Giovanni Montebello in Giarre, Mt. Etna, our friends at Murgo / Tenuta San Michele Winery in Santa Venerina & Nerello Mascalese. Thanks to Chiacchiri e Muddica, Antiche Botti, Sebastiano & Bondi Beach in Recanati, Sanctuary III @ il Terrazzo 54/B-fra il mare e la montagna. A lot of thinking and reflection occurred at aperitvi and cena in Roma at Wine Bar Baccanale with Armando and Aperol Spritz in the Campo dei Fiori, Trattoria da Luigi in Piazza Cesarini, and Osteria dell'Anima with Francesca off the Piazza Navona. I appreciate the ongoing support of my colleagues at the Università di Catania & Università degli Studi Roma Tre.

Publisher's Acknowledgments

Corwin gratefully acknowledges the contributions of the following reviewers:

Peter Dillon
Superintendent of Schools
Stockbridge, MA

Kate Anderson Foley
CEO
The Education Policy & Practice Group, LLC
Lakewood, OH

Sarah Johnson
Author, Speaker, and Administrator
Shell Lake, WI

Lena Marie Rockwood
High School Assistant Principal
Revere, MA

Ron Wahlen
Director of Digital Teaching & Learning
Durham, NC

About the Author

Christopher H. Tienken, EdD, is an associate professor of leadership, management, and policy and an education consultant. He has public school administration experience as a PK–12 assistant superintendent, middle school principal, director of curriculum and instruction, and elementary school assistant principal. He began his career in education as an elementary school teacher. Tienken is the former editor of the American Association of School Administrators *Journal of Scholarship and Practice* and the current editor of the *Kappa Delta Pi Record*.

Tienken's research interests focus on curriculum and assessment policy and practice at the local, state, national, and international levels. He was selected in 2019 as the Lead Author and Principal Investigator for the AASA Decennial Study of the Superintendent and was invited to be a member of the Professors of Curriculum organization in 2015. The Seton Hall College of Education and Human Services named him Researcher of the Year in 2014 and Tienken received the Truman Kelley Award for Outstanding Scholarship from Kappa Delta Pi in 2013. The Institute of Education Sciences recognized his research about the effects of professional development on student achievement and the National Staff Development Council (Learning Forward) awarded him the Best Research Award in 2008.

Tienken has authored over 80 publications including book chapters and articles. His third book, *Defying Standardization: Creating Curriculum for an Uncertain Future,* was awarded Outstanding Book by the Society of Professors of Education in 2019. His co-authored books include *The School Reform Landscape: Fraud, Myth, and Lies* with Don Orlich and *Education Policy Perils: Tackling the Tough Issues* with Carol Mullen. He presents papers regularly at state, national, international, and private venues. Tienken has ongoing research collaborations with colleagues at the Università degli Studi Roma Tre, Rome, Italy, the University of Catania, Sicily, and he was named as a visiting professor at both universities.

INTRODUCTION

A school leader colleague of mine once told me that, "Like it or not, standardized curriculum content is the law of the land now, and we have to implement it. I don't like it, but I have to roll it out and make sure the teachers teach it. What can I do?"

Many educators since then have shared that exasperated response with me in one form or another regarding education reforms. Whether it is teacher evaluation, high-stakes standardized testing, standardized curricular mandates, or the many other distally developed education reform proposals, some school leaders seem at a loss for ways to critique education reforms and determine how to take action if they believe a reform is potentially ineffective or how to capitalize on positive aspects of a reform. Many just "roll it out."

Creatively Comply!

My response to "It's the law, what can I do?" has always been not to blindly follow orders: "creatively comply!" Gain an understanding of the reform, and then customize it at the local level to benefit students, teachers, and stakeholders. Leaders must act in the best interest of their constituency. Regardless of the reform proposal or policy, school leaders have the power to mold it, shape it, delay it, repackage it, or try to circumvent it. Take a direction that keeps you and the school in compliance yet minimizes the negative aspects of the reform while accentuating the positive. Procrastinate on the rollout, and give teachers time to redesign their professional practice as a way to blunt the negative effects of the reform and enhance any positive aspects. Negotiate with the district for more support and resources for teachers and students. Circumvent the proposal, and do something better. All of the above? Do something!

History is replete with examples of leaders who followed orders based on questionable or bad policies instead of finding ways to lead in the cracks of those policies and creatively comply. In many cases, the lack of leadership is not because of a lack of a desire to lead. The desire is there, but perhaps the leader lacks a framework from which to understand the education reform landscape and lacks ideas on how to lead in the cracks and creatively comply.

Reform Defined

The term *education reform* as it used in this book aligns with the RAND Corporation definition of education reform as "any planned changes in the way a school or school system functions, from teaching methodologies to administrative processes." Specifically, this book focuses on education reforms that are mandated through a federal or state law or code or required via a formal school district or school policy.

Purposes

There are four main purposes for this book: (1) to provide a practical tool that school leaders can use to interpret and critique education reform issues within an ethical and evidence-informed framework, (2) to provide example critiques of four education reform topics that commonly result in more negative effects on students, (3) to present critiques of two education reform topics that result in more positive effects on students, and (4) to present ideas for how school leaders can ethically and creatively comply with education reform mandates to maximize the positive aspects and minimize the negative aspects.

Audience

The content of this book is aimed at school leaders but in the broadest of terms. The audience includes certified school administrators but also formal teacher-leaders and classroom teachers. The content is also relevant to parents, guardians, and community members who want to deepen their understanding of education reform issues and collaboratively participate in school decisions that result in positive experiences for all students. Finally, the content is appropriate for policymakers who wish to create evidence-based education policy.

Framing the Issues

Although readers will find many books on education reform, this book moves beyond reporting and commenting on reforms and brings together evidence-informed critique, ethical considerations, and creative compliance strategies in the form of a practical framework school leaders can use in their everyday practice. Anyone can admire a problem, but addressing a problem requires knowledge of effective education practice, leadership skills, and ideas for leadership. This book provides guidance for all three.

What This Book Supports

- Creative and ethical leadership that allows educators and students to thrive, **not just survive**

- Careful analysis and critique of reform initiatives before implementation

- Always putting students, students' needs, and students' social, emotional, and academic learning first

- Dedication to focusing on a few select reforms that are most likely to produce significant results in improving student learning: less is more

- Evidence-based practices

- School leaders who want to innovate and do the work necessary to ensure all students receive a quality education

What This Book Does Not Support

- The claim that all education reforms are bad or unnecessary; on the contrary, it advocates identifying the most promising reforms and focusing primarily on those.

- Resisting all reforms or resisting change—it is about actively and creatively leading schools to maximize good aspects of reforms and minimize the bad.

- Deceitful or unethical behavior

- Being an automaton and blindly following education mandates

Organization of the Book

The first three chapters form Part I of the book, and they present a practical framework from which school leaders can interpret and critique issues. The critique framework emanates from an evidence-based progressive/experimentalist Curriculum Paradigm as explained by Tanner and Tanner

(2007), based on the works of John Dewey and over 100 years of research from other selected progressive educators. The framework is founded upon (a) the historical purposes of public education in the United States, (b) the nature of how students learn best, (c) evidence-informed methods of organizing knowledge (the curriculum) so that all students can gain maximum benefit from the historic purposes of public education, (d) principles of human development, (e) ethical considerations, and (f) principles of creatively complying with laws and mandates to maximize the positive aspects of education reforms and minimize the negatives.

Part I provides school leaders with a contextual foundation for interpreting education reform within educational settings, ideas for ethical practice, and creative compliance strategies to overcome dubious reforms and capitalize on positive initiatives. Chapter 1 presents guiding principles of ethics that leaders can use as part of their moral compass. Chapter 2 provides seven specific strategies leaders can use to creatively comply with any education reform. Chapter 3 includes the practical framework tool and reflective questions school leaders can use to evaluate any education reform.

Progressivism is the philosophical buttress for the critique framework and the subsequent comments about the reform proposals in each succeeding chapter. Dewey (1916/2009) provided a progressivist definition of curriculum as the "reorganization of experiences (by students and educators) which adds to the meaning of experience and which increases ability to direct the course of subsequent experiences" (p. 57). It is incumbent upon school leaders to create "space" in the education program in which teachers can help students to connect the academic, social, and emotional content of school to themselves, other topics, and the world.

Cremin (1961) subsequently described broader principles of progressive education as the inclusive expansion of the programs and functions of schooling to encompass concerns about health, vocation, and community life, guided by pedagogy informed from evidence developed from the study of education issues and learning in education settings and customized to the students being served. Dewey's and Cremin's ideas require education to be customized at the local level, the point of contact—the school.

The practical framework presented in Chapter 3 bridges the gap between research and practice and provides school leaders with ways to critically discern the positive and negative aspects of a reform, creatively comply to maximize the good and reduce the bad, while still taking actions to customize the education experiences for all students.

The fourth through sixth chapters form Part II of the book and present readers with critiques and creative compliance strategies for three reforms that have historically included more negative aspects than positive. Chapter 4 addresses the umbrella issue of "rigor" as it pertains to education. Many of the education reform policies implemented since the inception of the No Child Left Behind Act (NCLB) of 2002 had the banner of rigor raised over them to justify their implementation. *Rigor* is a term that is often used but rarely defined. Chapter 4 takes a deeper dive into the term and provides a suggested definition based on evidence and ways school leaders can provide rigor without instilling conformity and standardization of thinking and learning.

Chapter 5 extends the discussion of rigor as part of a critique of the appropriate use of standardized test results. Depending upon in which state educators find themselves, the results from students' standardized tests can be used to judge the effectiveness of teachers, school administrators, the school as a whole, the school district, and also be used to determine school funding levels and the effectiveness of specific curricular programs. This chapter provides specific standards for the use of test results and gives educators concrete examples of how they can use their locally constructed assessments to arrive at reliable and valid decisions about student achievement.

Chapter 6 builds upon the previous chapter and critiques the policy of merit pay evaluation schemes for teachers and school administrators based on standardized test results. Approximately 40 states mandate the use of standardized test results as part of yearly teacher evaluations, and 29 states require their use for the evaluation of school administrators. Yet, the underlying theories of motivation and results from many large-scale experiments in the United States do not support the use of merit pay in general or the use of standardized test results to judge the effectiveness of educators. The chapter concludes with practical recommendations for educator evaluation and creative compliance strategies for school administrators to help alleviate some of the policy bite.

The final three chapters form Part III of the book and present reforms that historically have more positive aspects for students but have not been implemented consistently on a large scale. Chapter 7 provides an expanded view of traditional recess and leads readers into *Recess of the Mind* and mindfulness for increased student well-being. The chapter presents research and vignettes from several schools and districts about how they use recess of the mind. Chapter 8 presents problem-based and project-based learning as an evidenced-based method to unstandardize education and empower students and teachers to experience more equitable, effective, and socially conscious education. Chapter 9 contains a summary of the framework and ways to apply it to some of the most common recurring reform ideas.

Features of the Book

- Practical, evidence-based framework school leaders can use to critique education reforms to determine positive and negative aspects

- Seven specific, creative compliance strategies to maximize student and educator success

- Case studies that illustrate how to critique reforms and take action

- Reflective questions to guide critique and taking action

- An ethical decision-making checklist

Why I Wrote This Book

The impetus for writing this book came from my experiences as a former school administrator, a current professor of education leadership who helps prepare school administrators, and that of a parent of children in public school. As a principal, and then assistant superintendent, I was subjected to a steady diet of misguided policies from state education bureaucrats, and I needed a way to make sense of them on educational and ethical levels so that I could develop appropriate responses in order to shield, as best I could, teachers, students, and parents/guardians from any negative effects of bad policies.

As a professor, I see it as one of my duties to provide current and future school leaders a practical and evidence-informed toolbox they can use to interpret the multitude of policies and proposals they encounter so they can provide a quality, equitable education to all students and ensure a stable and professionally fulfilling education environment for teachers and parents/guardians.

Finally, as a parent, I was tired of watching school leaders jump on the junk science bandwagon and unquestionably implement every proposal that came down from the State Department of Education. Some school leaders seemed more concerned with self-preservation and earning "gold stars" from state bureaucrats than acting in educationally effective and ethically appropriate ways in the best interests of children. If they only had a framework and some ideas to help them lead better. . . .

Part I

REFORM CRITIQUE

Chapter 1

ETHICAL CONTEXT OF EDUCATION REFORM AND COMPLIANCE

Reform

The word *reform* when used in *education reform* often implies that something is broken and needs fixing. The rhetoric about the need to reform education in the United States is primarily based on the notion that America's entire PreK–12 public education system, one of the largest and most inclusive education systems in the world, is failing and needs to be fixed. However, the term *education reform* is rarely clearly defined by those who call for it.

The term *education reform* as used in this book aligns with the RAND Corporation's (n.d.) definition of education reform as "any planned changes in the way a school or school system functions, from teaching methodologies to administrative processes." Specifically, this book focuses on education reforms that are mandated through a federal or state law or code or required via a formal school district or school policy that an educator must lead, manage, or implement. *Education reform*, as it is used in this book, does not include things educators design or create themselves.

This chapter presents the first part of a three-part framework school leaders can use to discern the positive and negative aspects of an education reform and take action upon the reform to accentuate the positive influences and reduce the negative influences on students and educators. It focuses on determining the ethical disposition of education reforms and provides practical principles school leaders can use to reflect on the ethics of their proposed actions.

Ambiguous Rhetoric

Policies and programs enacted under the ambiguous banner of education reform are sometimes difficult to understand and critique. It is the ambiguity of the rhetoric used to justify the proposed education reform policies and programs that creates challenges for school leaders who try to determine the quality and efficacy of proposed reforms. In many cases, the rationales put forth for "reform" sound commonsensical but hide potential pitfalls for school leaders, educators, and students. For example, who would argue against more *rigorous* and standardized coursework for students so that they can all become *college and career ready* to better compete in the *global economy*? Why would educators not agree with programs that seek to reward them with a monetary bonus for raising student achievement on standardized tests? What could possibly be wrong with using results from standardized tests to judge student achievement, teacher quality, principal quality, and school quality and determine if a student can graduate high school or be promoted to the next grade? Why not give parents and guardians choices of how and where their children attend and receive education? Choice is democratic, isn't it?

It is the ambiguity of the rhetoric used to justify the proposed education reform policies and programs that creates challenges for school leaders who try to determine the quality and efficacy of proposed reforms.

Each of those questions is accompanied by answers that include positive and negative components, yet as Yong Zhao (2018) noted, the rhetoric of education reform never presents both sides; the potential negative side education effects of reforms are rarely ever noted. The ethical underpinnings of reforms receive almost no attention, as if the ends justify whatever means are necessary to achieve them.

Beneath the Crust of Rhetoric

On the surface, most of the reform rhetoric sounds appropriate and beneficial, and there are positive aspects to many of the education reform proposals. But the devil lurks somewhere below the surface, in the intricate details. Beneath the crust of the headlines and pious language live the issues of empirical support, implementation, and unintended consequences that are rarely fully examined or explained to educators or the public. In many ways, educators come to know the details as they are trying to implement the reform mandates. This can feel like flying a plane while simultaneously trying to build it.

Educators, and school leaders in particular, are sometimes put in the precarious position of having to react to the reforms at the point of contact: the school. They rarely have time to fully identify the intended and unintended long- and short-term consequences or to develop customized responses to the reforms prior to implementation, from the point of view of an organized critique derived from an evidence-based framework. The mountains of academic information, sometimes contradictory in nature, and confusing public rhetoric that accompanies each reform proposal can be overwhelming and difficult to decipher.

Educators, and school leaders in particular, are sometimes put in the precarious position of having to react to the reforms at the point of contact: the school.

The lack of an organized and evidence-based framework from which to assess reforms can leave some school leaders in the positions of supporting reforms that have long-term negative effects on students or not supporting reform proposals that would benefit students. School leaders should be able to make accurate judgments about education reforms in order to decide whether they must defend their students and educators from practices and policies built on nothing more than rhetoric, junk science, and anti-intellectual ideology or support a proposal or program founded on evidence of positive outcomes (Tienken & Orlich, 2013). Those judgments should be informed in part on the ethical characteristics of the reform.

Ethics Within the Context of Education Reform

School leaders can use ethical principles as part of a larger framework to assess and critique reforms and take action to blunt the negative effects of bad policies. This book situates ethics within dilemmas faced by school leaders in the acts of judging and implementing education reforms. School leaders must understand the ethical implications of enacting education reforms within the context of the reform and sphere of influence in which they lead. Stefkovich and Begley (2007) provided a general ethical guideline that school leaders should focus on the basic premise of working for students' best interests. This book takes that premise one step further and suggests that *evidence-informed* practice is a required part of ethical leadership. School leaders need to make an evidence-based determination as to whether the implementation of an education reform proposal is right or wrong, good or bad for students, educators, the school, the district, and/or the education system in general.

School leaders must understand the ethical implications of enacting education reforms within the context of the reform and sphere of influence in which they lead.

Starratt (1991) identified three types of ethics leaders can use to guide their actions: (1) the ethic of critique, (2) the ethic of justice, and (3) the ethic of care. The ideas, framework, and strategies presented in this book are situated within Starratt's three types of ethics yet draw upon the work of other experts in the domain of ethics. Starratt recommended that school leaders conduct reflection based on the order of critique, justice, and care.

Ethic of Critique

School leaders are presented with situations in which potential ethical conflicts can be difficult to discern. Organized critique provides the foundation school leaders can use to conduct ethical reflection on education reforms and their own responses to the reforms. Critique moves beyond superficial recognition of obvious details such as who must accomplish what. Critique provides school leaders with a way to examine deeply an issue or reform proposal from multiple perspectives, in an organized manner.

The critique framework presented in the first three chapters of this book provides school leaders with the following five perspectives from which to discern the positive and negative aspects of reforms: (1) the student, (2) the curriculum, (3) principles of human development, (4) social forces, and (5) ethics. School leaders are encouraged to work through all five perspectives when critiquing an education reform issue in order to better understand the potential positive and negative aspects.

Organized critique provides answers to three reflective questions whose answers will help inform future leadership actions (Buskey & Pitts, 2013):

1. In what ways does the reform further the purpose(s) of the organization?

2. Is the purpose of the reform generally ethically just, or are there inherent educational conflicts, and what are they?

3. How does the reform address or exacerbate inequalities in the system?

Ethic of Justice

The ethic of justice derives from two schools of thought. Starratt (1991) explained that one school promotes the idea that justice resides with the individual and not in social norms. He wrote, "Individual will and preferences are the only sources of value. Therefore, social relationships are essentially artificial and governed by self-interest" (p. 192). This school of thought about justice is decidedly self-centered and perhaps ill-suited for a democracy.

The second school of thought about the ethic of justice aligns with Deweyian views about the importance of the relationship between public school and a democratic society. It is only by participation in community life that individuals can fully come to understand how their own behavior influences the common good. Public school is the only publicly funded and universally accessible social institution that provides a mechanism to socialize all future adults to democracy. Ethical decision making undergirds acting for the greater good of society.

Public school is the only publicly funded and universally accessible social institution that provides a mechanism to socialize all future adults to democracy.

Sullivan (1986) clarified the relationship between community life and citizenship and democracy: "Citizenship is a shared initiative and responsibility among persons committed to mutual care" (p. 22). Understandings of justice flow from societal traditions and "present efforts of the community to manage its affairs in the midst of competing claims of the common good and individual rights" (Starratt, 1991, p. 192).

The focus of the individual's ethical development and decision making from the lens of a balance between community life and individual rights requires learning the responsibilities that individuals must assume in a democratic society to ensure that the rights and liberties of all people in the community are respected and protected. An ethic of justice proposes a constant search for homeostasis between the needs and wants of the individual and those of the greater good in a democratic society.

Starratt (1991) elaborated on the search for balance when he described two understandings of justice: (1) "justice as individual choices to act justly" and (2) "justice understood as the community's choice to direct or govern its actions justly" (p. 193). The two understandings of justice create a situation in which the choices of the individual are influenced by the choices of the community and vice versa, and the influences are reciprocal.

As Giles, McCutchen, and Zechiel (1942) wrote, "Individuals must learn that there are responsibilities, as well as advantages, in the sharing of concerns involved in group living" (p. 10). The ethic of justice, when viewed as a balance between the individual and the community, leads to the conclusion that a person's individual ethical interests do not supersede those of the greater good of the community. In the context of education reform, the ethic of justice requires school leaders to consider the intended and unintended impact of an education reform on themselves and on the larger education community and the system. An education reform could not be considered good or bad, right or wrong simply because it benefits or does not benefit an individual school leader. The reform must be judged in a larger context based upon evidence of how it impacts or will impact the community and the greater good.

Ethic of Caring

In general terms, the ethic of caring focuses on relationships between and among individuals. It moves the discussion of good or bad beyond contractual obligations and compliance with bureaucratic regulations toward recognizing the value and worth of people as individuals. Starratt (1991) explained,

> An ethics of caring requires fidelity to persons, a willingness to acknowledge their right to be who they are, an openness to encountering them in their authentic individuality, a loyalty to the relationship. (p. 195)

The ethic of caring requires that the right of the individual to be valued as a human being within the bureaucratic system must be upheld by individuals and the community. It is the ethical duty of those within a community to remain grounded in building a stronger community through human relationships, regardless of issues of efficiency, compliance mandates, effectiveness, or other issues that influence ethics within organizations (p. 195).

Starratt (1991) clarified,

> Such an ethic does not demand relationships of intimacy; rather it postulates a level of caring that honors the dignity of each person and desires to see that person enjoy a fully human life. (p. 195)

Finally, Starratt (1991) connected an ethic of caring to the importance of community within an ethic of justice:

> Furthermore, it recognizes that it is in the relationship that the specifically human is grounded; isolated individuals functioning only for themselves are but half persons. (p. 195)

The ethic of caring implies that to be a whole person, the individual must also participate in the community of relationships with others. In this way, justice and caring are linked in a system in which there cannot be justice without caring. In the education setting, ethics of caring require school leaders to take action and care for those within the system as much as it requires to care about them. Leaders must view the people within the system as human beings, not as inanimate objects such as test results, class sizes, duty coverage in school schedules, percentages on an academic growth chart, or annual teacher evaluation scores. Thus, the position set forth in the framework espoused in Chapter 2 is that school leaders must care about how an education reform will identify, label, define, or categorize the human beings impacted by it and then act to offset any potential negative effects in order to care for those in the system.

Social Justice and Caring

Noddings (1999) raised the claim that there cannot be justice without care, and both require action on the part of the leader. Noddings's position is supported by Gross and Shapiro's (2004) social justice perspective in which leaders take concrete actions to ensure people are afforded justice as a right, not something that has to be earned. Being a human should automatically afford someone the right to justice because that is fair. This view of the ethic of justice as fairness afforded through an ethic of caring has its roots in Rawls's (1971) idea of distributive justice. Noddings (1999) summarized Rawls's position on distributive justice as,

> people have rights; people are regarded as individuals; everyone should have a fair chance at securing desirable positions (equal opportunity); and if the rules cannot remove inequalities, they should at least be designed so that inequities favor the least advantaged. (p. 9)

School leaders should be on the lookout for reforms that restrict equity or advantage one group over another. They must be ready to act to increase equity through policies and practices that promote ethics of justice and caring.

> ## An Ethical decision-making checklist
>
> Eventually, the leader must decide whether to take action based on the initial critique. Those actions should be ethically just. Starratt (1991) provides four reflective questions leaders can use to examine one's potential actions:
>
> 1. How will my actions serve the greater good?
> 2. How will my actions respect individuals' rights?
> 3. How will my actions promote an ethical community?
> 4. How will my actions remove barriers to equitable education?

The Ethical Dilemma

Some education reforms enacted at the local school and district levels are state or federally mandated compliance measures. School leaders must implement them or face some type of formal punishment from the state education agency or the local school district or both. In some instances, compliance with faulty reforms or not implementing positive reforms could be unethical and educationally detrimental to students, teachers, or the system as a whole, which creates an ethical dilemma for school leaders. Is it unethical not to follow a law if the law includes unethical components?

For example, the Ohio State Board of Education instituted the Third Grade Reading Guarantee in which students who do not attain a specific cut score on a standardized reading assessment or subtest do not get promoted to Grade 4. Although the intent might be positive—to make sure all students can read by the end of Grade 3—the unintended consequences might be unethical. Consider that over 100 years of research suggests that retaining students in grade does not improve academic, social, or emotional outcomes. In general, outcomes for students are somewhat negative. What is a school leader to do?

Ethical Responsibility

Starratt (1991, 2004) suggested that school leaders view issues from three levels of ethical responsibility in order to help them resolve personal ethical dilemmas: (1) human being, (2) citizen, and (3) educational leader. Federal, state, and local education reform policies are in the domain of the educational leader, but Starratt asks leaders to consider the broader ethical picture—that of a human being and a citizen. The broader picture provides school leaders with the ethical cover to decide not to implement a reform policy or to attempt to revise the policy to be less unethical at the human being or citizen levels.

Reflective Questions for Ethical Decision Making

Ethical reflection is a strategy school leaders can use to ensure their ethical compass remains calibrated. School leaders can use the following questions distilled from Starratt's (1991, 2004) research on the three levels of ethical responsibility to formally critique the ethical disposition of a reform and help resolve situations in which they find themselves in a leadership ethical dilemma:

1. Level 1: Human being—How does the reform impact the recognition and respect of stakeholders' dignity as human beings and the right to exhibit unique characteristics and behaviors?

2. Level 2: Citizen—How is the greater good of students or educators in the local education community marginalized or enhanced by implementing the reform?

3. Level 3: Education leader—How do the intended or unintended consequences of the reform impact individuals, groups, or the educational community as it pertains to educational equity and social justice?

Try This!

Think of an education reform you are currently implementing or dealing with. Work it through the three reflective questions for ethical responsibility presented above to critique the general ethical dispositions of the reform. Did you find more negative or more positive ethical aspects, or was it split more evenly? What do your answers tell you about the ethical disposition of the reform and potential ethical dilemmas you might face?

Then answer the following two questions to critique the ethical dispositions of your leadership actions related to the reform implementation.

1. How do I know I am acting in ways that align with Ethics of Justice? What evidence do I have?

2. How do I know I am acting in ways that align with Ethics of Caring? What evidence do I have?

If your answers are uncertain or you don't have evidence, it might be time to take a deeper dive into your current actions in order to plan future actions that take into account the three levels of ethical responsibility within actions related to the ethics of justice and ethics of care.

Leadership Take-Away: Ethics

The ends or results of education reforms do not always justify the means or the methods used to attain them. School leaders must keep an eye on the broader ethical landscape and be mindful of practices, policies, and programs that violate ethical boundaries at the human being, citizen, and education leadership levels.

Next Steps

What can school leaders do when they recognize that compliance or noncompliance with an education reform is unethical or potentially educationally, socially, or emotionally harmful to students or staff? Each leader will ultimately be faced with situations in which the leader must decide whether it is more ethical to follow a reform that violates one or all of Starratt's three levels of ethical responsibility or choose to take a different direction. Leaders must also bring their own personal leadership ethical compass into the decision-making process on how to proceed.

(Continued)

(Continued)

School leaders may sometimes choose to creatively comply in order to do some good and less harm when implementing a reform they have determined to be ethically untenable. The next chapter offers seven specific creative compliance strategies school leaders can use to maximize the positive aspects of a reform while limiting the negative aspects.

Chapter 2

CREATIVE COMPLIANCE

When school leaders recognize that compliance with a reform mandate might cross an ethical boundary or not be in the best educational interest of all students, or they want to capitalize on a reform in a way that deviates from the mandated implementation, they may choose to engage in creative compliance. Creative compliance takes place when school leaders seek openings or cracks within the bureaucratic and legal structures of a reform where they can influence the implementation at the local level in order to do less harm, do more good, and maintain ethics of caring and justice within the educational community in which they lead.

> Creative compliance takes place when school leaders seek openings or cracks within the bureaucratic and legal structures of a reform where they can influence the implementation at the local level in order to do less harm, do more good, and maintain ethics of caring and justice within the educational community in which they lead.

Creative compliance has its roots in a concept known as creative insubordination (Buskey & Pitts, 2013), but it does not rise to the level of insubordination. It does not require outright disobedience, nor does it require school leaders to commit professional suicide or break the law. Creative compliance allows leaders to critique and consider paths of implementation rather than unquestionably or blindly following or implementing reform mandates imposed from above. Reforms do not have to be negative. They can be productive, creative, and innovative!

Creative Leadership Pathways

Creative compliance requires school leaders to seek out creative opportunities in which they take actions that limit the potential negative aspects of a reform, divert the trajectory of a reform in a more positive direction, or slow down implementation so that they can create opportunities for positive effects at the point of implementation: the classroom.

Dr. Ming Fang He (2016) described the need for school leaders to know why, when, and how to counter directives in ways that are politically savvy and guided by an ethical compass. One goal of creative compliance is to maximize the educational opportunities for all students and for the school leaders to live to fight another day for every student's right to a quality education and to protect every teacher's ability to provide a quality education. Outright subordination is not a preferred tactic because if school leaders commit professional suicide then students and teachers lose important voices in the long-term goal of providing quality education for all, and educators and their schools can be sanctioned.

Deceit Is Not the Intent

Creative compliance does not encourage or require deceitful behavior. It requires school leaders to understand the details of the reforms they implement and creatively search for ways to implement so that the positive aspects of each reform are maximized and the negative side effects are minimized. In some cases, school leaders must purposefully and strategically deviate from federal, state, or local guidance in order to maximize the positive aspects of a reform. Deviation need not be deceitful or unethical, but it should be strategic, creative, and informed by the best available information.

Seven Creative Compliance Strategies

The following seven strategies are purposefully broad because the tools a school leader uses to creatively comply, and how the leader deploys the tools, depends in part on the context of the reform, the context in which the school leader works, the ethical compass of the leader, the school leader's sphere of influence, and the overall political savvy of the leader. Leaders are not powerless in the face of mandated reforms. They can be leadership entrepreneurs and develop new ways to comply that are more effective than the well-trodden paths.

In some cases, it is easier to engage in creative compliance activities in larger districts, where there is less direct oversight at the school building level or district level. In other instances, it might be easier to comply

> creatively in smaller settings, where the superintendent, principal, or even teachers have more direct control over reform implementation efforts.

The seven strategies provide ideas from which school leaders can take ethical and evidence-informed educational actions to change the trajectories of negative reforms and capitalize on the strengths of positive reforms. It is important to remember that the overall goal of creative compliance is to take control of the reform and make things ethically and educationally better in the long run for teachers and students. Sometimes a solitary strategy will do, and in other situations, a leader might have to use several strategies together or take a layered approach. The leader must assess each situation to decide which strategy or strategies will be most effective at any given time.

Strategy #1: Crack the Code

Federal- and state-mandated education reform programs derive from legislation or state education code. A careful read of the legislation or code can sometimes identify loopholes or cracks that allow school leaders to comply in ways that limit some of the negative effects or accentuate the positive aspects.

In some cases, the secondary policy guidance memos put out by state education bureaucrats deviate from the actual state code and are more oppressive or restrictive than the code itself. Leaders need only follow the code. They can creatively comply within that code if they fully understand it.

The Curious Case of New Jersey

New Jersey state education code requires teachers to develop Student Growth Objectives (SGO) as one indicator of the state's three-part teacher evaluation system. Teachers must design two academic, quantitatively measurable SGOs per school year. According to the state administrative code, an SGO can be as straightforward as the following:

(Continued)

(Continued)

> *85% of Grade 1 students will demonstrate growth of at least two reading levels on the Fountas and Pinnell reading scale on a posttest administered in May compared to a pretest administered in September*. (Fountas & Pinnell, 2016)

The goal of the SGO must be based on previous data about student growth in the area selected by the teacher, and the SGO must be aligned to the New Jersey state-mandated curriculum standards. Beyond that, teachers have leeway to design, in consultation and with final approval by school administration, their SGOs as stated in the education code.

At the start of the second year of the SGO program, New Jersey education bureaucrats rolled out a new SGO design: the tiered SGO. A tiered SGO requires teachers to create multiple objectives within one SGO for different academic "levels" of students within their class. They distributed a policy guidance memo to all schools and held information sessions aimed at what they deemed as increasing the rigor of the process because it seemed to them that too many teachers were doing too well on their SGOs.

When changed to a tiered SGO, the example SGO above increases the chances a teacher will not attain the SGO goal because the tiers create more ways for a teacher to fail by creating more goals to achieve within smaller subgroups of students: (a) 85% of Grade 1 students reading a Level C on the *Fountas and Pinnell* reading scale in September will demonstrate growth of at least two reading levels on a posttest administered in May; (b) 85% of Grade 1 students reading a Level B on the *Fountas and Pinnell* reading scale in September will demonstrate growth of at least three reading levels on a posttest administered in May; and (c) 85% of Grade 1 students reading a Level A on the *Fountas and Pinnell* reading scale in September will demonstrate growth of at least four reading levels on a posttest administered in May.

When you split an already small group, let's say 25 students, into smaller subgroups, it is harder to show large gains because one student could count for as much as 20% to 25% of the subgroup score. If there are five students within a tier who must gain four reading levels in one year, and only one of those five does not, the teacher has not met the goal and appears to be a failure. The teacher must achieve all aspects of the tiered objective to get full points for the SGO.

School leaders in New Jersey unwittingly put their teachers in a situation that made it harder for them to show student growth if they blindly followed the nonbinding SGO guidance. This raised stress levels and lowered teacher evaluation ratings. It also caused some teachers to use more mechanistic teaching strategies the following year in the hopes of raising scores on tiered SGOs that were not legally required.

School leaders who read the education code carefully knew the bureaucrats had no basis for enforcing their requests and therefore ignored them. Instead, they helped their teachers to be more successful and feel less stressed by crafting high-quality SGOs based on good instruction. Those leaders used the power of code breaking (or better understanding the code) to empower their teachers and free them from stress that could get in the way of better teaching for students.

Leader Quick Tip

Strategy #1: Crack the Code Strategy

Good for: A reform or mandate supported by a law, administrative code, statute, guidance memo, and/or written policy

Not good for: Verbal mandates

Strategy #2: Procrastination

Procrastination (Hoy & Tarter, 2007) is one strategy that leaders can use to slow or blunt the potential negative effects of a reform while buying time to accentuate the positive. The pace at which a reform is implemented can be purposely slowed through raising questions, missing deadlines, forgetfulness, or simply waiting out portions or all of a reform until commanded or threatened to take an action. School leaders, and educators in general, can look for piecemeal procrastination openings within the totality of a reform in order to slow the process.

Procrastination at one point within a reform implementation sequence can cause ripple effects and buy time that can result in protecting stakeholders from the full brunt of a reform or providing openings to capitalize on positive aspects. Skilled school leaders and teachers are aware that most reforms change, evolve, or even die after one to three years. The bureaucrats who mandated the reform could change, or the law that brought about the reform could be amended, and thus the reform might disappear due to lack of organizational or political commitment.

Procrastination can be an effective tool to creatively comply and buy time to search for cracks within the education code or wait for the policy landscape to evolve or change. The time provided by procrastination can allow school leaders the opportunity to take actions that will result in better education experiences for all students and teachers.

Procrastination also gives time for the research community to catch up to the reform and provide additional data and information that school leaders can later use to oppose the reform or to support their recommendations about changes to the reform. It can take time for the fine-grained details about education reforms to emerge after implementation, and there are often times when the rhetoric does not match the reality. School leaders who jump on reform bandwagons without an understanding of the reform can find themselves looking the fool and harming students and teachers. The gift of time allows for better decision making based on more complete information and reflection.

Leader Quick Tip

Strategy #2: Procrastination

Good for: Reforms that lack rigid timelines or deadlines for implementation or reforms that do not have negative consequences for missing timelines or deadlines

Not good for: Reforms that have rigid timelines or implementation deadlines and have sanctions or negative consequences for missing timelines

Strategy #3: Tacking

Buskey and Pitts (2009) defined tacking as "strategies [that] involve simple actions designed to test the commitment of the system to the directives or to delay implementation until the situation changes" (p. 60). Tacking can include any actions school leaders use to divert attention and resources away from direct implementation of the reform they find to be unethical or educationally suspect and toward the positive aspects of the reform or toward changing the trajectory of the reform in order to do less harm. Tacking can be accomplished through acts of feigning compliance, like protracted inquiry or information gathering, the creation of study groups or ad hoc committees, stating a need for more skill development or professional development prior to implementing the reform, or attempts to refine or customize the reform at the district, school, or classroom level.

Undertaking actions that appear to enhance the reform but actually slow the implementation or divert the path can be used as tacking strategies. Such actions include reculturing the organization for reform prior to implementation, taking time to reskill staff through professional development programs in preparation for implementation, or conducting a potential problem analysis in which a bevy of organizational issues are uncovered that must first be addressed prior to implementation. Procrastination can be part of a tacking strategy, and it can be accomplished by actions that do not outright oppose the reform yet take the organization off a direct course of implementation or take extended time to accomplish.

Piloting

Piloting programs is one action that school leaders can use to tack. Piloting can narrow the scope of the reform, slow down full implementation, and potentially uncover fatal flaws that will make it politically untenable to persist with full implementation of the reform (Gutmore, personal communication, June 2018). Piloting also helps to find positive practices within a reform that can be highlighted. Piloting is the act of implementing a program on a smaller scale or pace. For example, instead of implementing a computer-based mathematics skill program with an entire school, a principal can propose implementing the program with one teacher per grade level for the first year and thereby buy some time and determine the merits and issues with program in a way that will produce data that the principal can then use to make a case for program revisions or termination.

Procrastination and tacking are less risky strategies for creative compliance in terms of possible negative repercussions against the procrastinator because procrastination and tacking can be camouflaged as compliance. Neither tacking nor procrastination require outright insubordination or overt opposition to reform. An advantage of both strategies is that they provide plausible deniability, or the ability for school leaders to deny acting in ways that would be seen as outright insubordinate. School leaders can point to authentic and necessary actions that they have identified as necessary precursors to successful implementation, or look like implementation, yet take time to accomplish on the way toward eventual implementation.

Leader Quick Tip

Strategy #3: Tacking

Good for: Reforms that do not have a rigid deadline for full implementation or benchmarks for success

Not good for: Reforms that have rigid timelines or deadlines for full implementation supported by benchmarks for implementation and sanctions or negative consequences

Strategy #4: Negotiation

Negotiation involves direct discussion with some level of the power source of the reform. It is a strategy that involves more potential risk for the leader compared to previous strategies. The negotiator aims to radically change the direction of the reform or abort the reform.

Let's Negotiate

A teacher can negotiate with an administrative supervisor regarding implementation aspects of a school-level reform. The teacher might negotiate more time to implement a program in an effort to procrastinate, betting that the reform will eventually go away or be replaced by another reform. The teacher might outright attempt to negotiate a complete lack of implementation by providing evidence that the reform will result in negative outcomes and providing a better alternative solution.

Similarly, a high school principal could negotiate with a superintendent about changes in the academic requirements that limit student access to higher level courses so that alternative criteria can be developed that are more equitable for students. Piloting is one alternative a principal can use during negotiations.

One risk of negotiation involves tipping one's hand or exposing one's intent or feelings about the reform and the strategies one might use to creatively comply. The teacher's or school leader's feelings or outlook about the reform might run contrary to those of their supervisors'. School leaders who consider negotiation should also have fallback positions and alternative ideas ready to use after negotiations fail in order to creatively comply and do no harm while also doing some good within the mandated reform.

The issues being negotiated, and with whom, are important considerations. There is little point in negotiating an aspect of the reform that cannot be changed or negotiating with someone who does not have the power to grant or effectuate the change. It would be pointless for a principal to negotiate with a superintendent to change the standardized testing mandated in the Every Student Succeeds Act (ESSA, 2015) that requires annual standardized testing in Grades 3 through 8 and once in high school in the areas of mathematics and English language arts. The testing requirement within ESSA is not a negotiable point.

However, that principal could negotiate the specific content and implementation of policies that the superintendent creates that voluntarily use test results from ESSA mandated tests to make important decisions about students, like whether to retain them in grade or admit them to specific academic programs. ESSA and most state education agencies do not mandate that student test results be used to make determination about grade retention or student access to academic programs. Therefore, a superintendent who voluntarily chooses to do so is also theoretically able to voluntarily retract such a policy. The superintendent has the power to propose policy changes or eliminate the proposal.

Code cracking can be an important tool when engaging in negotiations. The more a school leader understands the cracks that exist in a school reform mandate, the better that leader can negotiate because the leader will already know the openings that can be capitalized on during negotiations.

Code cracking can be an important tool when engaging in negotiations. The more a school leader understands the cracks that exist in a school reform mandate, the better that leader can negotiate because the leader will already know the openings that can be capitalized on during negotiations.

Leader Quick Tip

Strategy #4: Negotiation

Good for: Situations when the direct supervisor of the school leader would be sympathetic to negotiation or is on the same philosophical page with the school leader as it relates to the reform

Not good for: Situations in which the direct supervisor of the school leader is a "true believer" or ardent supporter of the reform or is not likely to consider positions other than his or her own

Strategy #5: Waivers

In the context of creative compliance, a waiver is something requested by a subordinate from a supervisor or government agency that allows the individual, school, or district to not implement the mandated reform but instead implement an alternative program in its place, aimed at accomplishing the same overall goal (D. Gutmore, personal communication, December 20, 2017). The waiver is formal approval not to implement the mandated reform, and it is akin to a permission slip to deviate from the original plan or mandate. Waivers can be part of a larger negotiation strategy.

Waive Me Through

A principal might ask a superintendent for a waiver regarding the implementation of a districtwide *writing across the curriculum* initiative that forces all teachers to use the same method. The principal could negotiate a waiver for the part of the program that requires all teachers to use the same method and instead propose a menu of methods that include the superintendent's preferred method but also allows for pedagogical creativity on the part of teachers to use other methods. The principal would prepare a formal request that includes the need for the waiver, a description of other methods, rationale for why the alternative methods will be more beneficial, an evaluation strategy, and timelines.

A waiver can be an attractive creative compliance tool because it provides formal consent to digress from the mandated reform. People tend to feel more at ease when they have formal approval to carry out their intended actions. Waivers can provide a sense of security and alleviate feelings of guilt that can sometimes be associated with strategies like circumventing.

Piloting can also be part of a waiver strategy if the leader cannot obtain a full waiver to not implement a reform. The leader can request a waiver from full implementation in order to conduct a pilot program based on the mandate. The leader can justify the request for a waiver to pilot a program by claiming the pilot program will improve the large-scale implementation and overall success of the reform.

Leader Quick Tip

Strategy #5: Waivers

Good for: Situations in which multiple options or methods exist to achieve the mandated goals

Not good for: Situations in which the entire method is mandated by a law, statute, or policy

Strategy #6: Circumventing

Buskey and Pitts (2009) identified another strategy that school leaders can use for creative compliance: circumventing. The authors defined circumventing as acts that people use to "work around the directives or change the nature of their implementation to mitigate the negative effects" (p. 60). One way school leaders can use circumventing as part of creative compliance is to customize the reform at the point of contact through any openings or cracks they find in the legal or bureaucratic aspects of the mandate through code breaking.

Returning to the SGO example introduced earlier, the evidence-based jury on the effectiveness of SGOs on influencing instruction and student achievement is not pretty. For the most part, SGOs don't have a tangible influence on long-term student achievement when controlling for other confounding variables like student demographics. SGOs can be overly burdensome to teachers and school leaders in terms of developing, implementing, and tracking results.

One strategy to circumvent the negative aspects of the SGO process is for the principal to help the teachers craft SGOs that are ethical, based on evidence-informed instructional practices, and meaningful to the teachers' specific classes but also highly achievable, so as to avoid any undue harm to the teachers' evaluation ratings or students' achievement. Code breaking reveals that state education code in most states that require SGOs allows for the collaborative development between the teacher and school leader. The school leader can circumvent the process by providing a menu of pre-written, highly practical, educationally effective, and achievable SGOs for teachers to choose from that comply with state regulations.

Leader Quick Tip

Strategy #6: Circumventing

Good for: Situations when the school leader controls the implementation actions and there is leeway for the leader to find cracks in the reform to change the overall trajectory while still meeting the mandate

Not good for: Situations in which implementation actions are rigidly prescribed

---

Strategy #7: Ingratiation

Ingratiation is a strategy that has been around since the invention of flattery. Leaders can use ingratiation to influence the decisions of a direct supervisor or power broker through actions that make the leader more likeable to the supervisor or power broker. Ingratiation can create the feeling on the part of a supervisor or power broker that the leader is "on my side" or "respects me," and those feelings can lead the supervisor or power broker to be more understanding and willing to view positively things like waivers, pilot programs, and negotiations. In some situations, the supervisor or power broker might even provide the leader with additional strategies for navigating the mandate.

Jones (1964) is often credited as having conducted landmark studies on ingratiation in the field of social psychology. Since then, the strategy has been refined to include several key behaviors that school leaders can apply separately or in combination (Grant, 2013; Stern & Westphal, 2010): (a) flattery as advice seeking; (b) indirect compliments to associates of the supervisor or power broker; and (c) referencing a common interest, affiliation, or colleague that aligns with the leader's position.

Providing flattery under the cover of advice seeking can help to disarm the supervisor or power broker and make him or her more amenable to feedback and alternative ideas. It can send a signal that the leader values his or her ideas, is willing to be vulnerable, and wants to collaborate. Camouflaging flattery as advice seeking also makes the approach less obvious and more likely to be accepted as authentic. It opens the door to later poking holes in ideas and questioning the supervisor's or power broker's ideas because the questions are posed within the context of collaboration, advice seeking, and learning.

Collaboration

Take the example of a state education bureaucrat who conducts a school monitoring visit and mandates that the district curriculum needs to be formatted to the preference of the bureaucrat because it is easier for her to review it in that format. Because the school leader already conducted code breaking, the leader knows the code only mandates the components that must be in a curriculum, not the format in which those components must be presented.

However, the bureaucrat holds the power because she conducts the final rating of the curriculum for monitoring purposes. The leader may say something like, "I really like that format because it is so much clearer and user friendly, but how do you recommend we get around the problem that the district did not budget for an entire curriculum rewrite this year and can't transfer any money for it? What do you think about us getting started right away on the curriculum that was approved during our budgeting process for this year, and then I will create a multiyear plan to get the others done according to your format and our budget constraints?"

(Continued)

(Continued)

This approach pokes a hole in this ridiculous bureaucratic request that an entire district's curriculum be rewritten without budgetary support, and it does so within a constraint that neither the leader nor the bureaucrat controls. It provides a smooth entry into the discussion with the ingratiation but then moves to the problem and provides an opportunity to find a workable solution proposed by the power broker that also buys time through what amounts to piloting a new format. Although the ultimate solution might not be the one the school leader wanted, it is a solution.

Communicating indirect compliments to associates of the direct supervisor or power broker is another strategy to curry favor. They are positive comments made about the supervisor or power broker to associates who will most likely inform that person. Indirect compliments can work to create positive impressions about the school leader, that in turn can help to bring about positive relationships and make the supervisor or power broker more likely to listen to concerns and accept alternative ideas.

School leaders can use indirect compliments before and after meetings with supervisors or power brokers to create positive impressions from start to finish. The key for the school leader is to know what to say and which people to say it to. In the example of the state education bureaucrat who mandated a specific curriculum format, a potential indirect compliment before the initial meeting could focus on how the school leader has heard that the bureaucrat is very knowledgeable and has great ideas about curriculum writing and that the school leader is looking forward to getting good advice. The leader might comment to the same person about how helpful the bureaucrat was following the meeting, how the ideas about curriculum writing were informative, and how the leader looks forward to working with the bureaucrat again. In this way, the leader bookends the encounter with compliments and positive impressions.

Referencing a common interest, affiliation, or colleague that aligns with the leader's position to a supervisor or power broker is another way to build a positive affiliation and send a message that you have common interests. People are more likely to take suggestions and accept alternative ideas from people with whom they think they share common interests. Common interests also help to build a sense of trust and familiarity, which in turn can add perceived validity and greater acceptance to any points or arguments the leader makes later.

The pros of ingratiation include relationship and trust building; however, this is a strategy that requires tact and skill. The line between ingratiation and flat-out deceitful brownnosing is a thin one, and brownnosing is easy to identify and can be viewed as insincere and erode trust. Ingratiation requires skill and should not be attempted without fully understanding the risks of failure.

Compliance Entrepreneur

Creative compliance often requires the use of more than one strategy. Just as some business entrepreneurs seek out new uses or customize existing products to repurpose them, so too can school leaders become entrepreneurial in the ways they creatively comply and repurpose reforms to meet the needs of their students. Although creative compliance strategies rest on a base of science, it is an art in terms of their implementation. One must know which strategies to use and when. Figure 2.1 summarizes the situations in which a leader might best apply each.

Finding the openings and cracks within which creative compliance can flourish requires an understanding of the educational potential of the reform and whether it is rooted in sound evidence in practice. Evidence-informed critique can provide that understanding.

Failure Is an Option

Although prior proper planning increases the chances that things will work out the way you want them to, there can be times when your strategies

Figure 2.1 • The Seven Strategies—When to Use Them, When Not to Use Them

Strategy	Good For	Not Good For
1. Code Cracking	Reform or mandate supported by a law, administrative code, statute, guidance memo, or written policy	Verbal mandates
2. Procrastination	Reforms that lack rigid deadlines for implementation and do not have negative consequences for missing deadlines	Reforms that have rigid deadlines supported by sanctions or negative consequences
3. Tacking	Reforms that do not have a rigid deadline for full implementation	Reforms that have rigid deadlines for full implementation supported with negative consequences
4. Negotiation	Direct supervisor of the leader is sympathetic to negotiation or is on the same philosophical page with the leader as it relates to the reform	Direct supervisor of the school leader is a "true believer" or ardent supporter of the reform or is likely not to consider positions other than his or her own
5. Waivers	Multiple options or methods exist to achieve the mandated goals	Method is mandated by a law, statute, or policy
6. Circumventing	School leader has control of the implementation actions and leeway exists to find cracks in the reform to customize implementation to change the overall trajectory and still meet the mandate	Situations in which implementation actions are prescribed
7. Ingratiation	Leaders with positive reputations who are viewed as sincere and have experience with ingratiation or have personalities that lend themselves to ingratiation in ways that are believable	Leaders who are not comfortable with flattery, small talk, or inauthentic interpersonal relationships

do not work. School leaders should always consider what can possibly go wrong with their ideas and plan for failure (R. Andrews, personal communication, February 21, 2019). They should engage in potential problem analysis (Kepner-Tregoe, Inc., 2013).

Potential Problem Analysis

1. Identify the potential problems (not symptoms).

2. List the most likely cause for each potential problem.

3. Develop a preventive action plan based on the cause.

4. Develop a contingent action plan (Plan B) in case your preventative action plan does not work.

Try This!

Think of an education reform you are currently implementing or implemented in the past in which creative compliance strategies could have improved it. Answer the following questions:

1. Which strategies did you use?

2. Why did you choose those strategies?

3. Would your trusted colleagues feel the same way about this reform and your method of creatively complying? If not, why? What can you learn from them, or what can they learn from you?

4. How did you ensure that you did not cross into deceit or unethical behavior?

5. What potential problems do you foresee, and what can you do about them now and for a Plan B?

Leadership Take-Away: Creative Compliance

Mixing aspects of creative compliance tactics can result in new ways to do good while living to fight another day in whatever context a leader works.

Next Steps

The ethic of critique requires school leaders to discern the positive and negative educational aspects of a reform. It is difficult to creatively and ethically comply when one does not understand the educational efficacy of a reform. Leaders must act, but those actions must be informed by facts.

Chapter 3 presents an evidenced-informed, practical framework school leaders can use to critique education reform proposals. The framework brings together ethics and considerations for creative compliance within a framework for education quality. The framework is rooted in progressive/experimentalist philosophy and is organized around sets of questions that are rooted in the empirical literature related to education best practices, ethics, and creative insubordination. The framework is presented as a tool to help school leaders make better sense of education reforms and better decisions about how to proceed with implementation and compliance.

Chapter 3

REFRAMING REFORM

Reframe It!

Most education reform proposals and policies are developed without substantive educator input, and students are rarely, if ever, included in meaningful ways within the policy development process. School leaders are often placed in the position of reform receiver, not reform developer, and they are often mandated to implement policies and practices that they had no hand or voice in shaping. Therefore, it is imperative that school leaders have a framework that helps them critique the ethical and educational efficacy of reforms so that they can lead in ways that help to maintain an ethic of justice, an ethic of caring, and educational quality at the point of implementation: the classroom.

Most education reform proposals and policies are developed without substantive educator input, and students are rarely, if ever, included in meaningful ways within the policy development process.

Purpose

This chapter presents a practical, evidence-informed framework that school leaders can use like a set of reflective lenses to operationalize the ethic of critique and evaluate reform proposals and to devise evidence-informed strategies from which to base creative compliance and ethical actions. The framework contains six lenses school leaders can use to critique education reforms and then act upon them: (1) the historical purposes of public education in the United States, (2) the nature of learning, (3) theories of human development, (4) the nature of knowledge and effective ways to organize curricula and experiences, (5) ethics of care and justice, and (6) strategies for creatively complying with education reforms (Dewey, 1916; Tanner & Tanner, 2007). The chapter culminates with a Desk Reference of the

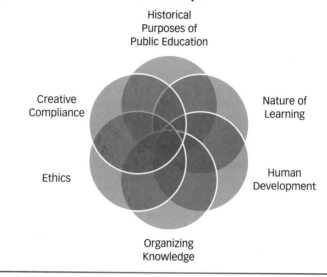

Figure 3.1 • **Six Lenses of Critique**

Historical
Purposes of
Public Education

Creative
Compliance

Nature of
Learning

Ethics

Human
Development

Organizing
Knowledge

Top 10 critique questions school leaders can use to implement the framework on a daily basis.

Research-Based and Action Oriented

The critique framework derives from the progressive philosophy and the Curriculum Paradigm explicated by Tanner and Tanner (2007). The first four lenses rest upon landmark research from the likes of Lester Ward (1883), John Dewey (1902, 1916), Wilford Aikin, (1942), Hilda Taba (1962), Ralph Tyler (1949), and other progressive thinkers from the 19th and 20th centuries, and it is bolstered by recent findings from the field. The remaining two lenses incorporate theories and research from perspectives of ethics and creative compliance in the education setting to provide school leaders with tools to help consider actions necessary to ensure a quality and equitable education for all students. The framework provides leaders with a way to begin to answer the question, "What can I do?"

Reflective Leadership

It is reasonable to expect educators to determine the potential efficacy of the reform proposal or program so they can, as Dewey and Tufts (1908, p. 2) described, make determinations between whether the reform is ethically and educationally "right and wrong, good and bad" for students, educators, and the system as a whole. School leaders must decide the level of compliance they should pursue after understanding the intended and unintended educational and ethical ramifications of an education reform proposal.

Framing Reform

Education reform policies and programs do not operate in isolation. They are part of a societal ecosystem. Therefore, a critique framework should take into account the cultural and practical contexts in which educational policies or programs are implemented. Because almost all education reform policies and programs eventually directly or indirectly impact students in classrooms, special attention should be paid during the critique process to the eventual downstream consequences to students: the *So What?* or bigger picture of education reform.

Because almost all education reform policies and programs eventually directly or indirectly impact students in classrooms, special attention should be paid during the critique process to the eventual downstream consequences to students: the *So What?* or bigger picture of education reform.

The first four lenses of the framework provide tools to determine the big picture of educational efficacy, or the *So What* of education quality. The lenses rest upon the landmark research that forms what is known as the Curriculum Paradigm (Tanner & Tanner, 2007). The fifth lens focuses on deciphering the ethics of a reform. The sixth lens represents the *Now What?* or creative compliance actions leaders must take to ameliorate any negative effects of reforms or capitalize and extend positive aspects without sacrificing their jobs and future ability to lead.

Curriculum Paradigm

The Curriculum Paradigm is founded upon the progressive philosophy of education and almost 150 years of results from empirical research and informed professional practice. Progressivist philosophy is grounded in egalitarian and democratic processes through the "reorganization of experiences which adds to the meaning of experience and which increases ability to direct the course of subsequent experiences" (Dewey, 1916/2009, p. 57). Egalitarianism is based on the idea that everyone should be afforded equal treatment and equal access to a society's social mobility apparatus in order to lead a productive and sustaining life (Roemer, 1998).

One useful characteristic of the Curriculum Paradigm is that it provides guidance to educators who might not know how to specifically understand an education issue or how to design a response to best meet the needs of students and teachers. The paradigm provides direction to educators to help them design creative, evidence-informed policies and practices that are more likely to benefit those impacted by them.

A Framework for Critique

A framework for critique of education reform proposals, policies, and practices must acknowledge the historical purposes of public education because the historical purposes help leaders to understand the big picture context in which education operates. Trying to understand how education reform ideas fit into the public education context without acknowledging the historical purposes of the public education system is like trying to steer a sailboat without understanding the purpose of a rudder. It becomes an effort in drifting and leaves the boat at the mercy of the ocean currents and winds.

Purposes of Public Education

Public education in the United States has historically had three specific aims. The aims were translated into three complimentary functions of the public school macrocurriculum, the vehicle to accomplish the aims, as first described by Lester Ward in 1883 and later expanded upon by John Dewey (1916/2009) and the authors of the Cardinal Principles of Secondary Education (Commission on the Reorganization of Secondary Education, 1918) and others. The three historical aims of education are to prepare students for life economically, sociocivically, and avocationally.

The three historical aims of education are to prepare students for life economically, sociocivically, and avocationally.

The economic aim of education should provide students with a general set of knowledge and skills they can use as a platform to progress to specialized education needed for a career and economic independence. Many education reforms have been aimed at standardizing curriculum content as a means to increase economic viability. Economic viability and standardization do not have to go hand in hand. Standardization of content and academic outcomes does not beget better economic results, and it can stifle creativity and innovation (Tienken, 2017). Results from studies conducted during the last 100 years suggest that curricula should be (1) informed by evidence, (2) based on needs of students and the larger society, and (3) unstandardized and problem-based in order to fully equip people for economic viability.

The sociocivic aim includes the knowledge and skills that help students become responsible and participating citizens in a democracy and the global community. One historic role of public education has been that of the incubator of democratic thinking in the United States (Dewey, 1959). Public education has a history of uniting diverse peoples through exposure to a liberal education. Dewey (1929) explained the importance of the sociocivic role of public education in nurturing a democracy:

> For the creation of a democratic society we need an educational system where the process of moral intellectual development is in practice as well as in theory a cooperative transaction of inquiry engaged in by free, independent human beings who treat ideas and the heritage of the past as means and methods for the further enrichment of life, quantitatively and qualitatively, who use the good attained for the discovery and establishment of something better. (p. 84)

Education reforms that violate basic tenets of sociocivic learning pose a threat to democracy, and school leaders need to be able to recognize those threats and respond to them. Likewise, leaders need to exploit reforms that are more egalitarian in nature and promote democratic principles and increase equity for all students.

The avocational aim of education is accomplished through the knowledge, skills, and experiences that help students develop their personal interests, passions, and hobbies (Dewey, 1916; Tanner & Tanner, 2007). Public education should help people develop into well-rounded human beings so they can improve their communities, cultures, country, and the larger global community (Commission on the Reorganization of Secondary Education, 1918). Of course, there are indirect benefits to the economic function of education when people are exposed to other pursuits. People generally become more cognitively nimble, culturally literate, personally satisfied, and socially conscious when exposed to diverse ideas and experiences, and those dispositions help them in their careers (e.g., Aikin, 1942; Zhao, 2018).

Within the three aims of the public school curriculum there have been two overarching purposes of the public education system itself: unifying and specializing (Commission on the Reorganization of Secondary Education, 1918). The public education system is the mechanism to unify a diverse population around the tenets of an egalitarian and participatory democracy and provide programs in which students can go on to specialize their academic interests and individual passions to support pursuits of an economic vocation and personal growth.

The development and specialization of the individual is not to be confused with individualism. One cannot lose sight of the big picture of democracy in terms of individuals contributing to the greater good of their local communities, larger American society, and the global community. Giles, McCutchen, and Zechiel (1942) warned of confusing individual development with individualism:

> The development of the individual as a goal is not to be confused with individualistic action as a method for its achievement. Unrestrained individualism is inconsistent with democratic values since it will not guarantee others the realization of their potentialities . . . a sharing of responsibilities are essential for the development of personalities to their maximum. (p. 10)

The development and specialization of the individual is not to be confused with individualism. One cannot lose sight of the big picture of democracy in terms of individuals contributing to the greater good of their local communities, larger American society, and the global community.

One focus of an individual's development is learning that there are responsibilities that one must assume in a democracy to ensure that the rights and liberties of all people are respected and protected. The development of one individual cannot impinge upon or retard the growth of another. "Individuals must learn that there are responsibilities, as well as advantages, in the sharing of concerns involved in group living" (Giles et al., 1942, p. 10).

The authors of Volume II of the Eight Year Study (Giles et al., 1942) combined the three complimentary functions of public education into two categories and described the purposes of public education to address the needs of the individual and society:

In this definition of purpose, two broad guiding principles are evident: (1) the educational program should aid the learner in making effective adaptation to his environment in all its major aspects physical, economic, and social; (2) the educational program should develop in each individual those personal characteristics that will enable him to participate effectively in the preservation and extension of the culture. (p. 5)

Policies and programs that do not align with the historical aims of public education or violate democratic principles and traditions generally do not provide for greater equity. They are generally authoritarian in nature and imposed upon the system from external forces, through the use of coercion and legal mandates. They more often favor certain groups over others. The favored groups are usually members of the ruling class. Dewey (1897) made his thoughts clear on the topic of undemocratic reforms when he wrote, "all reforms that rest simply on the enactment of a law, threatening of certain penalties upon changes in mechanical or outward arrangements are transitory and futile" (p. 80).

Reflecting on the Historical Lens?

So What? reflective questions allow educators to gain a sense of how the reform fits into the historical context of education in terms of what existed in the past and why, what has been tried in the past and the results of those efforts, and how to use the past as a guide to improve the future.

The following is a *So What?* question that school leaders might ask when reflecting on a reform as it relates to the historical aims of education:

1. How well does the/would the reform address the three historical aims of education for students, and what can I do about it?

Leader Quick Tip

If the answer to any of the questions is "not well" then the leader needs to look for cracks in the reform where he or she can apply creative compliance strategies to improve the situation. If the reform is well positioned as it relates to the questions, then the leader must look for ways to capitalize on those strengths to get the maximum educational bang for the reform buck.

Principles of Human Development

The second lens of the critique framework is based on principles of human development. Although widely attributed to psychologist Jean Piaget, the concept that human cognitive development occurred in stages was first described by John Dewey in his writings produced between 1899 and 1910, well before Piaget's work, and later refined in writings up through 1938 (Tanner, 2016). Dewey (1899) concerned himself with cognitive development in the context of education, and hence, his identification of stages of development comes from work with children in actual educational settings, schools, and not clinical settings like the work of Piaget.

Dewey identified four stages of cognitive development, with three of those being relevant to formal school. Dewey described the first stage from ages zero to four as the pre-operational stage of growth. However, he labeled the first stage of development related to education as beginning at age four, presumably because formal schooling begins around that age:

> The first stage, found in the child say of from four to eight years of age, is characterized by directness of social and personal interests, and by directness and promptness of relationship between impressions, ideas, and action. (pp. 97–98)

In Dewey's description of the next stage of development, the fluid nature of cognitive development is apparent:

> the aim is to recognize and respond to the change which comes into the child from his growing sense of possibility of more permanent and objective results and of the necessity for the control of agencies for the skills necessary to reach these results. . . . The mere play of activity no longer directly satisfies. It must be felt to accomplish something, to lead up to a definite and abiding outcome. (p. 99)

Dewey (1910) included reflective thinking as his final stage of cognitive development within the educational setting: formal operations of thought. For instance, students thinking about the problems associated with their proposed solutions to a socially conscious problem adds a purposeful reflective aspect to a learning situation. Reflective thinking provides openings for students to consider and evaluate the consequences of their decisions and to weigh various options against criteria.

Reflective thinking provides openings for students to consider and evaluate the consequences of their decisions and to weigh various options against criteria.

Reflection need not be reserved only for those students perceived as cognitively advanced. Asking students to reflect on how mathematical computation can be used to help others, or how the world would be different without the concept of subtraction, are forms of reflection that are accessible to all students. Dewey (1916/2009) commented that "every end becomes a means of carrying activity further as soon as it is achieved" (p. 77). The learning never ends. Reflection creates openings for educators to extend learning (Woolfolk & Perry, 2011).

Cognitive development is contextual and fluid. A student might be able to think abstractly in consistent ways in some topics or subjects, depending on his or her prior experiences with the subject matter, whereas the same student might not be able to conceive of another topic in abstract terms because of a lack of prior experiences. Not all humans arrive at exactly the same developmental point at the same time.

Some students arrive at formal operations several years before their peers. Similar to how some children walk at 10 months, whereas others might not walk until 13 or 14 months, doctors do not put the nonwalking 12-month-old child in special remedial walking classes or deem the child not "sports-ready" for the rest of the child's life just because the child did not walk at the exact time period that some other children took their first steps. It is important for school leaders to recognize that differences in student output might simply reflect individual differences in the pace of developmental and prior experiences and not be indicative of a student's life potential or future ability.

Likewise, policies and programs that provide opportunities for educators to reflect on their practices beget better design and implementation of those programs and policies.

Professional reflection leads to what Maslow (1943) identified as self-actualization, the point at which a person is operating at optimal levels of independence and self-efficacy by finding meaning in personal life and work. Achilles, Reynolds, and Achilles (1997) termed it "constant-renewal," in the context of organizational change. Constant-renewal is a stage of the change process in which people are innovating and customizing policies and programs in ways that were not imagined and thereby bringing additional value to the policy and practice.

Educators can find themselves at various stages of professional development or readiness for various policies and practices. Novice teachers, teachers who change grade levels or subject area teaching assignments, or teachers who leave the profession for several years and then return can all have varied levels of professional development needs. Education reform proposals need to be flexible enough to allow those who possess more readiness for the content of the new proposal to move forward while also providing those who might be less ready with more time to develop the skills and dispositions necessary for implementation. School leaders need to create that flexibility when they determine that it does not exist but should.

The following is a *So What?* reflective question that school leaders can ask to critique an education reform proposal based on principles of human development:

1. What are the implications of the reform for those inside and outside the range of the developmental stage upon which the reform is predicated, and what can I do about it?

The Nature of the Learner

Results from classic and recent studies about how students learn best coalesce around a theme of active learning. The essence is that students learn best when engaged in learning opportunities and experiences that recognize the nature of the learner, the student, as an active constructor of meaning who brings life and academic experiences, interests, passions, emotions, and prior collateral knowledge to the classroom (e.g., Gijbels, Dochy, Van den Bossche, & Segers, 2005; Kontra, Lyons, Fischer, & Bellock, 2015; Prince, 2004). The learning situation should allow the learner to connect his or her prior experiences to the new content or skills and use those experiences as a bridge to more learning.

> Results from classic and recent studies about how students learn best coalesce around a theme of active learning.

The experiences and knowledge students possess might be based on traditional academic content or based on life experience, but research has proven for a long time that no student is a passive blank slate, empty vessel, or sponge (e.g., Thorndike, 1924). Prior experiences of the student cannot be ignored or jettisoned from the learning environment because those experiences provide the potential bridges between the student's existing knowledge and skills. Dewey (1916/2009) noted that educators must abandon the notion of education as the pouring of "knowledge into a mental and moral hole which awaits filling" (p. 39). Education policies and practices should capitalize on opportunities to connect content to students through developmentally appropriate common experiences, interests, passions, and emotions to inform the content and organization of the curriculum.

The learning of professional educators shares some similarities with aspects of child learning in that there is ongoing reconstruction of knowledge, reflection on experience, and innovation of expertise that enables the educator to hone skills and exercise more intelligent decision making and methods over subsequent educational contexts and situations. Educators connect their present actions to prior experiences and learning, and they use them as springboards for new actions and innovations to address the fluid situations of teaching. Reforms must allow for that and provide leeway for educators to take active roles in the customization of implementation.

The following is a *So What?* reflective question school leaders can ask related to the nature of the learner:

1. How well does the reform acknowledge the target audience (e.g., student, teacher) as an active constructor of meaning who brings prior knowledge to the situation, and what can I do about it?

School leaders must identify opportunities and methods to promote active involvement on the part of students and educators when they recognize that a reform does not promote it. Equally, leaders must work to capitalize on the active involvement of educators and students to increase equity when a reform provides openings to do so.

Organizing the Knowledge

Organizing the knowledge of education relates directly to the design, development, and implementation of curricula. Distally developed curriculum content standards are the cache of current education reform policies and programs. Standardized expectations for student re-creation of predetermined knowledge and skills, presented in predetermined formats, act as the skin and bones of the rhetoric of college and career ready standards. Organized in discipline-centered silos such as mathematics, language arts, or history, the content standards are then dispensed in their silos to students in regular doses as mandated by state laws and school district curriculum pacing guides.

However, evidence from over 100 years of the study of curriculum problems in public education provide educators with another conception of how knowledge should be organized to maximize student cognitive, moral, and social development. The evidence suggests that knowledge should be organized as a fusion of discipline-centered subject matter and personal/societal experiences, as the means to connect the content to student experiences, interests, and prior knowledge.

> The evidence suggests that knowledge should be organized as a fusion of discipline-centered subject matter and personal/societal experiences, as the means to connect the content to student experiences, interests, and prior knowledge.

Historically, students achieve better academic, sociocivic, and avocational results when knowledge is organized into socially conscious, problem-based, and project-based curricula activities (Dewey, 1916; Jersild, Thorndike, & Goldman, 1941; Taba, 1962; Thorndike, 1924; Tienken, 2017). In most cases, the more customized the curricula is around relevant problems and projects of interest to the students, the more opportunities and multiple pathways students have to self-actualize their learning and achieve better results on academic and affective measures (Tienken, 2017; Wang, Haertel, & Walberg, 1993; Zhao, 2018).

From the standpoint of the school leader in the current reform context, discipline-centered content such as algebra, biology, and U.S. history exist, and leaders must ensure the content is taught. One problem with many curricular-based education reforms is that the content is divorced from student experience and organized as separate bundles of information to be received by students.

Although regulations require educators to administer the mandated content, there is still some degree of autonomy over how to package the mandated products. Leaders must look for the openings in reforms where creative autonomy can be exercised. Policies and programs that seek to script educator practice or restrict educators' ability to design, develop, and customize curriculum would be critiqued as less effective within the proposed.

> Although regulations require educators to administer the mandated content, there is still some degree of autonomy over how to package the mandated products. Leaders must look for the openings in reforms where creative autonomy can be exercised.

The following are some *So What?* reflective questions related to organizing knowledge:

1. How well does the reform allow the organization and delivery of knowledge to be customized to maximize active learning and participation of the target audience?

2. How well does the reform provide for the connection of the mandated content or process to the existing knowledge and skill set of the target audience?

Reforms that mandate rigid methods of design and implementation or do not allow for customization at the local level will require creative compliance actions to change the trajectory of the reform at the point of contact: the school. Leaders must seek out and capitalize on opportunities that allow for the customization of implementation.

Once school leaders gain a better understanding of the educational details of the reform proposal, they must also confront the ethical issues of reform. They must come to a determination of whether the reform, as mandated, meets the basic tenets of the ethics of justice and care.

Ethical Evidence

School leaders must consider whether implementation of the reform violates or aligns in some way to the ethics of justice and the ethics of caring. Ethics-related questions school leaders should consider in their critique include the following:

1. How does the reform impact the recognition and respect of stakeholders' dignity as human beings and the right to exhibit unique characteristics and behaviors, and what can I do about it?

2. How is the greater good of students or educators in the local education community marginalized or

enhanced by implementing the reform, and what can I do about it?

3. How do the intended or unintended consequences of the reform impact individuals, groups, or the educational community as it pertains to educational equity and social justice, and what can I do about it?

Now What? and Creative Compliance

In some cases, leaders must apply creative compliance strategies if they find issues that contradict the educational or ethical lenses of the framework or want to capitalize on aspects of a reform that are otherwise being overlooked or not supported. The creative compliance lens of the critique framework provides the opportunity for school leaders to take action. It is the opportunity for school leaders to answer the prompt, "Because I know this now I should . . ."

Now What? and Moving From Passive Receiver to Active Leader

The answers to the Creative Compliance *Now What?* questions help to move the school leader from passive recipient of reform to active customizer of practices and policies. Instead of simply admiring the problem, the questions within the creative compliance lens prod school leaders to take the next step and take evidence-informed action about the issues they identified with the reform.

The *Now What?* questions in the creative compliance lens direct leaders toward actions and methods that can creatively address areas of the education reform proposal found to be out of alignment with the critique framework or capitalize on positive aspects.

School leaders can use the entire framework to design and implement evidence-informed strategies in ways that save them from committing professional suicide and allow them to live to fight another day for children and the larger community while doing some good.

The following are some *Now What?* questions school leaders can use to guide their thinking about creative compliance:

1. What creative compliance strategies can I take within my sphere of influence that will help to revise the education reform or capitalize upon it to become more aligned with the Curriculum Paradigm and the ethics of justice and care, in order to do less harm and more good?

2. What creative compliance strategies can I use to slow or blunt the education reform, if necessary, so as to create space from which to change the proposal to become more aligned with the Curriculum Paradigm and the ethics of justice and care at the point of contact with students or educators?

Leadership Take-Away: Framing Reform

One cannot be a leader in title or position only. One must lead, and leadership requires action. Leaders must be able to know what actions to take and why they are taking them. The Top 10 Critique Questions provide leaders with an organized method to operationalize the critique framework on a daily basis.

Figure 3.2 • Top 10 Desk Reference Critique Questions

So What? Reflection Reference	
Historical Purposes of Education	**Human Development**
1. How well does the/would the reform address the three historical aims of education for students, and what can I do about it?	1. What are the implications of the reform for those inside and outside the range of the developmental stage upon which the reform is predicated, and what can I do about it?
Nature of Learning	**Organizing Knowledge**
1. How well does the reform acknowledge the target audience (e.g., student, teacher) as an active constructor of meaning who brings prior knowledge to the situation, and what can I do about it?	1. How well does the reform allow the organization and delivery of knowledge to be customized to maximize active learning and participation of the target audience, and what can I do about it?

(Continued)

Figure 3.2 • **(Continued)**

So What? Reflection Reference
2. How well does the reform provide for the connection of the mandated content or process to the existing knowledge and skill set of the target audience?

Ethical Evidence

1. How does the reform impact the recognition and respect of stakeholders' dignity as human beings and the right to exhibit unique characteristics and behaviors, and what can I do about it?

2. How is the greater good of students or educators in the local education community marginalized or enhanced by implementing the reform, and what can I do about it?

3. How do the intended or unintended consequences of the reform impact individuals, groups, or the educational community as it pertains to educational equity and social justice, and what can I do about it?

Now What? and Creative Compliance

1. What creative compliance strategies can I take within my sphere of influence that will help to revise the education reform or capitalize upon it to become more aligned with the Curriculum Paradigm and the ethics of justice and care, in order to do less harm and more good?

2. What creative compliance strategies can I use to slow or blunt the education reform, if necessary, so as to create space from which to change the proposal to become more aligned with the Curriculum Paradigm and the ethics of justice and care at the point of contact with students or educators?

Try This!

Now it is your opportunity to put it all together and operationalize the critique framework presented in the first three chapters. Reconsider the issue you reflected on for the Try This! exercise in Chapter 2. Run it through the Top 10 Desk Reference Critique Questions.

- What educational issues or opportunities did you find?

- What potential ethical dilemmas do you anticipate, and how would you ensure that you do not cross from ethical creative compliance to deceit?

- What do you know that you do not know, and who will you call upon from your coalition to fill in the blanks?

- What creative compliance strategies will you use, and why?

Next Steps

The multidimensional framework proposed in this chapter brings together educational, ethical, and creative compliance considerations that allow school leaders to develop a deeper understanding of education reforms, discern the ethical implications of implementation, and plan evidence-based actions to do more good and less harm. Figure 3.2 provides the questions for each lens of the framework that educators can use as a desk reference to conduct a critique of education reform proposals.

Parts II and III of the book present case studies of five education reforms. Part II contains three controversial education reform topics based on dubious empirical evidence, and Part III presents two positive reforms based on methodologically sound research and practice. Each case provides an evidence-informed critique based on the framework presented in the first two chapters.

Leaders can use the examples presented in the next five chapters to learn more about some of the most controversial and promising education reform topics and to sharpen their own skills of critique, creative compliance, and ethical leadership. Although other frameworks for critique exist, the one presented in this chapter brings together a mix of components to evaluate the merits of a reform within the context of educational efficacy, ethics, the historical purposes of education, and creative compliance.

Part II

REFORM CASE STUDIES

Chapter 4

CASE STUDY 1
Reframing Rigor

This case study illustrates how the generic term of *rigor* can be misused in education reform and provides readers with an evidence-based definition and example of how to apply the critique framework to better understand rigor and capitalize upon it to improve education for all students.

Origins of Rigor

Rigor is a term that has steadily made its way into the lexicon of education reform. Some salient examples include products like the Common Core State Standards (CCSS) and national standardized tests. For example, the corestandards.org website claimed that the CCSS were "based on rigorous content" (National Governors Association & the Council of Chief State School Officers, 2017). Similarly, the vendors of the Partnership for Assessment of Readiness for College and Careers (PARCC, 2014) described the PARCC test items as "of sufficient quality and rigor." Although widely used, rigor is rarely defined, and it is often misunderstood, which causes reforms to be misguided.

The term *rigor* did not appear in the original Elementary and Secondary Education Act (ESEA) of 1965 (PL 89-10), but the 1994 reauthorization of the ESEA, known as the Improving America's School Act of 1994 (PL 103-382), seems to be the first piece of large-scale Title I federal education legislation in which the term *rigorous* appears. *Rigorous* was used seven times in the act.

The Goals 2000: Educate America Act of 1994 (PL 103-227) included the terms *rigor, rigorous*, and *rigorously* eight times. The 2002 reauthorization of the ESEA, known as the No Child Left Behind Act (NCLB; PL 107-110), signed by President George W. Bush in 2002, included the words *rigor* and *rigorous* 29 times throughout the legislation. Finally, the 2015 reauthorization of the ESEA, known as the Every Student Succeeds Act (ESSA; PL 114-354), included the term *rigorous* 31 times.

What Is Rigor?

There does not seem to be agreement on what constitutes rigor in K–12 education policy-making definitions. An unscientific poll conducted by the Hechinger Report (2010) asked 20 education experts and policymakers, university presidents, professors of education, directors of corporate divisions of education products, state governors, and school district superintendents and other educators and policymakers to define the term.

There does not seem to be agreement on what constitutes rigor in K–12 education policy-making definitions.

The poll revealed 20 different definitions, but the majority of the definitions tended to focus narrowly on academics and equated rigor with the amount of effort required by a curriculum standard or task. Little mainstream literature has been put forth regarding rigor as a type of thinking required or engendered by curriculum, and it is the development of higher-level thinking that educators should pursue in order to meet the three historical purposes of education.

Defining Success

A lack of a unified definition makes it impossible to set metrics for successful creation and implementation of rigorous curriculum or evaluating student accomplishment of rigorous work. This chapter presents an argument that educators should rethink rigor to make the term more productive and less apt to be misused. It puts forth a definition of rigor related to the type of thinking fostered by a curriculum standard or task, not the perceived difficulty.

Common Confusion of Rigor

Many empirical and nonempirical studies of "rigor" related products, like the CCSS or various commercial standardized tests, often equate rigor with difficulty, not the complexity of the thinking required by students. Porter, McMaken, Hwang, and Yang (2011) used the Survey of Enacted Curriculum to examine the degree of content alignment and content

CHAPTER 4

difficulty between the CCSS and previous content standards from selected grade levels from 27 states. The study focused on the difficulty of the expectations related to the content, not the type of thinking fostered by the standards, yet the results and recommendations have been equated to rigor.

Similarly, the authors of the nonpeer-reviewed report from the private think tank The Thomas Fordham Institute confused difficulty with rigor when they wrote, "the level of rigor is appropriate for the targeted grade level(s). Students are expected to learn the content and skills in a sensible order and an appropriately increasing level of difficulty" (Carmichael, Martino, Porter-Magee, & Wilson, 2010, p. 357).

Carmichael et al. (2010) created their own system to rank standards based on their definitions of clarity, content, and rigor. The authors equated rigor with difficulty in the rubric they created to judge the standards. Thus, their conclusions are based solely on the difficulty of the content, not the type of thinking required. The nuance lies in the fact that difficult content does not always equate to complex thinking. The differences are important for the long-term cognitive growth of students.

Redefining Rigor

It is the focus on how knowledge is selected and used for democratic means that brings the conception of rigor full circle and to the point of a possible working definition for education in a democratic society: original thinking that includes connections among existing knowledge and created knowledge, which could eventually lead to the taking of democratic action or to the proposal and reflection of solutions to societal problems. The degree to which a curriculum standard, task, assessment question, or learning objective fosters such thinking determines its rigor. The definition acknowledges rigor as something that resides in the realm of complex thinking, regardless of difficulty.

Original thinking includes connections among existing knowledge and created knowledge, which could eventually lead to the taking of democratic action or to the proposal and reflection of solutions to societal problems.

Complexity Versus Difficulty

Dewey (1916/2009) described two different types of knowledge that students can experience in school settings: higher level and lower level. In Dewey's conception of higher level knowledge, there is a purpose for thinking and learning, and that purpose is for taking action: using knowledge to solve a socially conscious problem. Socially conscious problem solving requires complex thinking: the interaction of academic content knowledge and active use of personal experience to generate original solutions.

Although the conceptions of complex thinking in education are diverse, there appears to be a general theme in the research literature: Complex thinking includes purposeful, original thinking on the part of the student that can result in different outcomes or solutions. In most cases of divergent thinking, there is not a predetermined answer that the curriculum standard presupposes. Complex thinking is more divergent than thinking aimed at remembering something, literally comprehending material, or following a prescribed process.

Difficult Is Not Complex

Difficulty is a static component of a learning objective or curriculum standard that refers to the amount of effort or work a student must expend to complete a task, and it frequently manifests itself in lower level thinking. Dewey (1916/2009) described low level knowledge when he wrote,

> Frequently it (knowledge) is treated as an end itself, and then the goal becomes to heap it up and display it when called for. This static, cold-storage idea of knowledge is inimical to educative development. It not only lets occasions for thinking go unused, but it swamps thinking . . . Pupils who have stored their "minds" with all kinds of material which they have never put to intellectual uses are sure to be hampered when they try to think . . . everything is on the same dead static level. (p. 114)

Leader Quick Tip

A curriculum standard that requires students to solve a multistep addition problem, in which students use answers from each step, arrived at via computation based on recalling and applying a standard algorithm to inform each successive step, represents difficulty, not complexity. Students must simply apply a memorized procedure, multiple times. There is not original thinking involved; there are just more steps and

(Continued)

more effort required. The complexity of thinking resides at the recall and imitation of procedure levels for each step of the problem.

Solving multistep computation problems represents static thinking: recalling information from cold-storage to arrive at predetermined answers. Regardless of the amount of effort it takes a student to solve, the multistep addition problems do not engender complex thinking.

Goldilocks View of Rigor

Equating rigor with difficulty presents a problem in which universally mandated curriculum standards or learning tasks can be too hard, too easy, or just right, depending on the background knowledge and prior experiences of the students. Take, for example, an English language arts sample test item from a Grade 10 national standardized test that uses a short story excerpt set in Japan. Some of the language is culturally related to Japan, including references to aspects such as red cranes and Japanese maple trees in autumn. Several of the sample questions deal with word usage and definitions.

> Equating rigor with difficulty presents a problem in which universally mandated curriculum standards or learning tasks can be too hard, too easy, or just right, depending on the background knowledge and prior experiences of the students.

Students with more life experiences and prior knowledge of Japan or horticulture might find these types of questions *just right* on the Goldilocks scale of rigor. But students who have never left their town or live in environments that do not have Japanese Maple or deciduous trees, do not experience a change of seasons, or do not have exposure to literature set in Japan or other parts of the Asian continent might find the tasks too hard.

The level of thinking embedded in the Grade 10 test question does not rise above the literal comprehension level, and it simply requires students to identify predetermined answers. There is no original thinking or action being taken on the part of the students. Although the item is said to represent rigorous content by the test manufacturer, the thinking required by the student is not complex; it is literal comprehension based on difficult text, due to inclusion of difficult and unfamiliar vocabulary.

Conversely, a conception of rigor based on complex thinking creates a situation in which the standard or task is purposefully designed in a way that is *just right* for all because students are required to use original thinking and produce a response at the level of sophistication at which they are ready to produce at that time. Regardless of the sophistication of the response, the level of thinking required for all students is complex.

For example, a Grade 5 complex standard requires, "Proposes hypothetical actions based on the perceived potential for impact" (Asia Society, 2015a, p. 2). Some students will produce proposals for this standard that are simplistic and do not take into account multiple variables that could affect the impact, whereas other students might produce multiple actions based on combinations of potential variables and their impact. Regardless of the sophistication, the standard requires all students to engage in complex thinking because they must use original thinking. Original thinking and synthesizing a response from multiple subject areas is required, and there is not a predetermined answer.

Creative Thinking as Complex Thinking

Lewis and Smith (1993) seemingly channeled Dewey's conception that complex thinking is related to solving perplexities when they explained that complex thinking occurs when a person takes new information stored in his or her memory and rearranges or extends the information to achieve a purpose or find possible answers to perplexing situations. In this way, complex thinking can be conceptualized as a nonlinear form of thinking, based on a purpose that often generates multiple possible solutions to a situation.

Sternberg (1999) connected creativity to complex thinking and explained that creativity is "the aptitude to generate work that is unique and original as well as suitable for the specific task or problem one is attempting to solve" (p. 3). Sternberg's conception places creativity in the context of complex thinking that is original thinking, used for a specific purpose.

Albert and Runco (1999) introduced a humanizing function as part of the purpose for complex and creative thinking:

> The early conceptualizations of creativity and research were in themselves exceptional creative acts, as was the eventual bridging of these concepts through deliberately applying research

methods. These methods were essential not only to the meaning and significance of creativity in human experience, but to why and how historical events were set in motion. (p. 16)

Albert and Runco's (1999) conception situated complex thinking as an active and purposeful aspect of human development and societal progress and not just a static state of being or remembering. Runco and Jaeger (2012) extended the conception of complex thinking when they synthesized that original thinking needs to lead to some effective outcome to be considered complex.

Based on Albert and Runco's (1999) and Runco and Jaeger's (2012) syntheses, creative and complex thinking would be somewhat meaningless if they did not lead to some kind of effective progress for life. The idea of thinking for progress harkens back to Dewey's (1916/2009) explanation of the power of socially conscious problem solving in which students engage in studying, proposing, testing, and reflecting on solutions to complex problems of society.

Collaboration and Complex Thinking

Padget (2013) extended creative thinking beyond the individual with the contention that creative and complex thinking should be thought of as a collaborative effort: "most modern human achievements are the result of teamwork; groups of individuals, like jigsaw puzzles of different coordinated talents and aptitudes, experiences and enthusiasms" (p. 22).

Padget's conception of complex thinking connects to the historical sociocivic aim of education because it includes student use of collaboration and communication in the curriculum to inquire about and take action upon social problems. Although the conceptions of complex thinking in education seem to be diverse, there appears to be a general theme: Complex thinking includes purposeful, original thinking on the part of the student that can result in different outcomes.

Although the conceptions of complex thinking in education seem to be diverse, there appears to be a general theme: Complex thinking includes purposeful, original thinking on the part of the student that can result in different outcomes.

Complex Curriculum Standards

If one views rigor as related to complex thinking, then rigorous curriculum standards or tasks should allow for multiple conceptions and multiple answers to the same question, based on students learning and applying knowledge for the purposes of taking action upon a socially conscious problem.

The following Grade 10 curriculum content standard from the Asia Society Center for Global Education (2015b) fosters complex and open-ended thinking and allows for more collaboration, communication, and complex thinking around a social problem on the part of students: "Identifies opportunities for personal or collaborative action to address a situation, event, issue or phenomenon in a way that is likely to improve conditions" (p. 2). The standard provides opportunities for students to use knowledge in original ways for the purpose of solving a pressing issue.

Rigor in the Context of Democracy

It is the fostering of complex thinking through the study of socially conscious problems that helps to incubate democratic thinking and democracy itself. Rigor must serve to forward humanistic conceptions when defined in the context of a democracy. "Democratic society is peculiarly dependent for its maintenance upon the use in forming a course of study of criteria which are broadly human" (Dewey, 1916/2009, p. 138). Dewey (1916/2009) rejected the selection of content knowledge for solely utilitarian purposes. He wrote, "Democracy cannot flourish where the chief influences in selecting subject matter of instruction are utilitarian ends narrowly conceived for the masses, and for the higher education of the few, the traditions of a specialized cultivated class" (p. 138).

Results From Studies of Complex Thinking

Results from classic studies based on the effects of complex thinking, specifically found in problem-based curricula, include those from Aikin (1942) and Jersild, Thorndike, and Goldman (1941). The results support the importance of defining rigor via complex thinking because complex thinking situations increase academic achievement and one's ability to transfer knowledge to solve problems. Difficult thinking alone does not.

Aikin reported the results from the landmark Eight Year Study and found that graduates from 30 high schools in which the curricular program focused on complex thinking via socially conscious problem solving outperformed peers in traditional high schools on all academic and social measures in college. The Eight Year Study followed 2,500 matched pairs of students over an eight-year period through high school and college. According to a follow-up study 20 years later, the students also outperformed peers on other life indicators as adults (Willis, 1961).

Jersild et al. (1941) included tens of thousands of high school students in New York City who received an activity curriculum embedded with complex thinking and compared their achievement to students involved in traditional curricula. Students in the "activity schools" outperformed their peers from traditional schools on standardized tests of academic achievement, although the students from the traditional schools possessed higher pre-achievement scores than the students from the activity schools.

A large body of recent work exists as exemplified by Pogrow's studies of the influences of the Higher Order Thinking Skills (HOTS) program for students in Grades 4 through 8 (1998, 2004). Pogrow's HOTS curricula focused on providing students consistent opportunities to use original thinking in general problem situations not directly related to a school subject. Results from Pogrow's studies based on HOTS being used in over 2,500 schools during the last 35 years suggest that general complex thinking strategies in which students have consistent opportunities to use original thinking raise student achievement in content areas.

Functional Fixedness and Knowledge Reproduction

Students can experience what Runco and Chand (1995) call "functional fixedness" (as cited in Ward, Smith, & Finke, 1999, pp. 201, 247) when they receive a steady diet of non-\complex education experiences, regardless of how difficult the content is for them. If a set of curriculum standards does not have a mix of cognitive complexity students have fewer opportunities to gain the consistent learning experiences they need to think in complex ways.

Student thinking can become rigid or stunted if they receive a predominance of low-level, convergent or declarative and procedural thinking opportunities (Runco & Chand, 1995; Sternberg, 1999).

Student thinking can become rigid or stunted if they receive a predominance of low-level, convergent or declarative and procedural thinking opportunities.

Runco and Chand (1995) defined functional fixedness as "the rigidity or mental set that locks thinking so an individual cannot see alternatives" (p. 247). Curriculum content standards focused on lower level and convergent thinking do not have the divergent thinking opportunities needed to develop cognitive flexibility and can lead to functional fixedness.

Dewey (1916/2009) described that an intense focus on knowledge reproduction and imitation can lead to a lack of deep learning needed to apply knowledge in authentic situations:

> We can and do supply ready-made ideas by the thousand; we do not usually take much pains to see what the one learning engages in significant situations where his own activities generate, support, and clinch ideas, that is, perceived meanings or connections. . . . If he (the student) cannot devise his own solution (not of course in isolation, but in communication with the teacher and other pupils) and find his own way out, he will not learn, even if he can recite some correct answer with one hundred percent accuracy. (p. 115)

If the limitations of functional fixedness are understood during the creation of curriculum standards, then standards, substandards, activities, and assessment items can be designed to potentially increase cognitive "originality and flexibility," by ensuring that a mix of cognitive complexity is embedded throughout the standards in each subject and for each grade level (Runco & Chand, 1995, p. 245).

So What? Understanding the Big Picture of Rigor

This section provides leaders with an example critique of rigor as viewed through the reflective questions from five of the six lenses of the critique framework.

1. How well does the proposed expanded definition of rigor forward the historical democratic aims of public education, and what can I do about it?

Figure 4.1 • Five Lenses of Critique

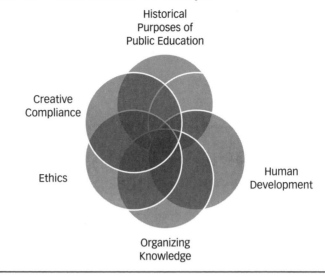

Historical
Purposes of
Public Education

Creative
Compliance

Ethics

Human
Development

Organizing
Knowledge

The expanded definition as proposed in this chapter recognizes the socio-civic and economic functions of public education, and as such, aligns more closely with the three historic purposes of public education in the United States: (a) economic, (b) sociocivic, and (c) avocational. The definition allows for the intersection of academics, socially conscious use of the academics, and personal development for the greater good. The proposed definition facilitates a rebalancing of reform priorities toward the student and the historic purposes of public education.

Conversely, the mainstream idea of rigor based on difficulty focuses on only a narrow conception of the economic function of education and difficult content. No major federal education reform since the NCLB era has had an explicit focus on the sociocivic or avocational purposes of education or complex thinking.

2. How well does the definition of rigor proposed in this chapter acknowledge the nature of the learner as an active constructor of meaning who brings prior knowledge and experience to teaching and learning situations?

The expanded definition places the learner in the role of an active participant in the learning process and aligns better with the nature of learning explicated in the Curriculum Paradigm (Tanner & Tanner, 2007) described in Chapter 3. Because the proposed definition links rigor to complex thinking, and one hallmark of complex thinking is the use of original and reflective thinking on the part of the student, the student has the opportunity to move from passive receiver of knowledge to active constructor of knowledge and reconstruct his or her learning experiences.

If the initial conception of the learner is someone who actively makes meaning from content and uses that meaning to create new solutions to problems, then curricula and associated learning activities must place the student and the educator in the roles of knowledge creators, more so than knowledge imitators. Definitions of terms influence how knowledge is organized for learning.

3. How well does the proposed definition provide for the connection of the new knowledge or skills to the existing knowledge and skill set of the target audience?

The definition proposed in this chapter fosters the organization of knowledge around socially conscious problems that allow students to connect and use their prior knowledge and experience as springboards for new learning and to take action and reflect upon their actions. The focus on original thinking provides opportunities for students to connect content to themselves, the world, and other subject matter, adding the possibility of interdisciplinary and life connections to the curriculum.

The student uses existing knowledge and skills and new content knowledge and skills for the purpose of solving socially conscious problems. The student is action-oriented, not subservient to the content as a passive receiver in the education process. The student-centered nature makes the content relevant to the world of the student because the student uses content to act upon the world. The proposed definition facilitates the development of truly relevant and rigorous education experiences for all children and increases educational equity in the process.

The proposed definition facilitates the development of truly relevant and rigorous education experiences for all children and increases educational equity in the process.

4. What are the implications of the reform for those inside and outside the range of the developmental stage upon which the reform is predicated, and what can I do about it?

CHAPTER 4

Dewey (1899) noted, "Now we believe in the mind as a growing affair, and hence as essentially changing, presenting distinctive phases of capacity and interest and interest at different periods" (p. 34). Dewey's insight about human cognitive development occurring in stages has been demonstrated as fact in the 100-plus years since his declaration. Thus, any education reform proposal or policy derived from a call for greater rigor must acknowledge that cognitive development is not a finite endeavor. Children do not all master the same developmental stages at the same time or in the same manner.

Human development is naturally accounted for within the proposed definition of rigor because rigorous tasks need to include open-ended aspects that allow for original thinking. Original thinking is naturally differentiated by readiness because students produce output at levels of sophistication at which they are ready, based on prior experiences and background and the connections they are able to make between new learning and prior knowledge and experiences.

The dividing lines between rigorous and nonrigorous curricula and tasks can be more easily determined with a definition that includes complex thinking instead of difficulty. Difficulty is a relative concept, and as such, cannot be applied universally across a curricular program to describe rigor. Complex thinking exists empirically. It can be defined, identified, and applied universally.

Difficulty is a relative concept, and as such, cannot be applied universally across a curricular program to describe rigor. Complex thinking exists empirically. It can be defined, identified, and applied universally.

CHAPTER 4

Ethical Considerations

5. How does the reform impact the recognition and respect of stakeholders' dignity as human beings and the right to exhibit unique characteristics and behaviors, and what can I do about it?

A myopic focus on rigor as difficulty, without recognition of the value of complex thinking in the service of socially conscious issues, can create a situation in which students are not valued for divergent thinking. When the focus is on one right answer, wrong answers, original thinking, or answers that are not expected can lead to the student being labeled as not proficient or not capable of doing rigorous work. The labeling can lead to the student being placed in a remedial program and becoming a "basic skills kid" or a "bubble kid" (Booher-Jennings, 2005) or a student who is close to reaching proficiency on a state test and thus given more test prep attention in order to pass.

Viewing students through only one academic lens and categorizing them based on that lens has the potential to dehumanize them. There is more than one way to be "smart," but the current definition of rigor relegates academic "smartness" to getting unduly difficult questions correct. Education should be a process of discovery, a discovery of one's self and one's relationship with subject matter and society. It should be the process of trying to find what cannot be found.

Creative Compliance and *Now What?*

The evidence-based definition of rigor offered in this chapter provides an enlarged view of academic proficiency and allows various types of thinking to be valued and align better with the ethic of justice. Perhaps, if leaders work to expand the definition of rigor they will also expand options for students to be considered more successful and less frequently labeled as a category of student and more frequently valued for the unique individuals they are.

Perhaps, if leaders work to expand the definition of rigor they will also expand options for students to be considered more successful and less frequently labeled as a category of student and more frequently valued for the unique individuals they are.

---

1. What creative compliance strategies can I take within my sphere of influence that will help to revise the definition of rigor to capitalize upon it and become more aligned with the Curriculum Paradigm and the ethics of justice and care, in order to do less harm and more good?

In a case in which leaders are forced to implement a new program in the name of a myopic view rigor, they must first determine what type of thinking the program requires. Because most programs brought into schools are not tested for their efficacy in terms of fostering complex thinking, school leaders must conduct their own evaluation of the program to determine the thinking requirements.

Circumventing

In cases in which programs lack complex thinking, school leaders can use circumventing to work with their staff to customize the program at the point of implementation: the classroom. School leaders can support teachers to modify activities or objectives to include more complex thinking, or to "go off the script," if teachers are mandated to use robotic scripted programs. School leaders can also circumvent myopic rigor by allowing teachers to change the amount of time students spend on programs that foster convergent thinking. School leaders can also circumvent by providing teachers with additional resources to enrich programs dominated by low-level thinking.

Piloting as Procrastination and Waivers

School leaders can request to pilot a program they determine to be based on difficulty, yet dominated by low-level thinking. A one-year pilot with a smaller group can help delay launching into full-fledged use of an untested program with all students. Piloting will slow down the initiative and allow time to collect data to show superiors the detrimental effects of the program and to substantiate the need for customization at the local level or even justify a waiver from implementing the program. Piloting limits any negative effects of an untested program to a smaller number of students, and a waiver can provide the official approval to proceed in a different direction.

Cracking the Code on Complexity

Leaders must be able to determine the rigor of the programs and activities they use with students. Various frameworks exist to help leaders crack the code of complexity and difficulty within curriculum content standards, programs, and assessments. Some of the most common frameworks to help leaders include Hess's Cognitive Rigor Matrix (Hess, Carlock, Jones, & Walkup, 2009) and Webb's Depth of Knowledge (1997).

School leaders can work with teachers to use complex thinking frameworks and determine, with a good deal of accuracy, the percentage of standards or test questions or classroom activities that require complex thinking and those that do not, as has been done in recent studies of the CCSS that found a preponderance of low-level complexity and difficult standards (e.g., Sforza, Tienken, & Kim, 2016). Then educators can make the decision to add more rigorous standards and activities to their local curricula that actually improve student thinking.

Hess's Cognitive Rigor Matrix attempts to capitalize on the strengths of Bloom's Taxonomy of Educational Objectives (Bloom, Engelhart, Furst, Hill, & Krathwohl, 1956) and overcome some of the main weaknesses of the taxonomy by combing Bloom's cognitive levels with Webb's Depth of Knowledge (DOK) framework. Hess's Cognitive Rigor Matrix provides practical examples of how Bloom's levels that are commonly denoted as higher level (e.g., analysis) can actually produce low-level thinking by requiring a predetermined answer. Hess's Cognitive Rigor Matrix is a helpful tool for educators to design activities after complex thinking standards have been developed.

Webb's DOK contains four levels. Levels 1 and 2 represent less complex declarative and procedural thinking, whereas Levels 3 and 4 represent strategic and extended levels of complex thinking. The DOK helps to describe the type of thinking required by a standard or task, not the likelihood that the task will be completed correctly or the amount of effort required to complete a task or meet the performance expectations of a standard (Webb, Alt, Ely, & Versperman, 2005).

Try This!

- What are some examples in which rigor is defined as difficulty in your setting, and what can you do about it?

- What ethical dilemmas are created?

- Which creative compliance strategies can you use, and why?

- What opportunities exist to capitalize on rigor or redefine it so that it increases educational opportunities and quality for all students?

- What potential problems do you foresee, and what can you do about them now and for a Plan B?

Leadership Take-Away: Rigor

Redefine rigor and enlarge the curriculum to include original thinking and action-oriented activities. Do not be fooled by proposals masquerading as rigorous but based on difficulty and narrow definitions of academic achievement.

Chapter 5

CASE STUDY 2

Using or Abusing Standardized Test Results?

This case presents school leaders with clarity about limitations of standardized test results from the point of view of interpretation validity. Current practices of test interpretation are critiqued, and suggestions to improve professional practices through creative compliance strategies are presented.

Large-Scale Use

Large-scale use of commercial standardized tests in the United States began around 1918 with the introduction of the U.S. Army's Alpha and Beta tests of intelligence. The tests were meant to efficiently screen, sort, and select recruits for Officer Candidate School and aid in the sorting of recruits into specific occupations within the army during World War I (Brandwein, 2011a, 2011b). The U.S. Army administered the tests to approximately 1.75 million recruits during World War I.

Standardized testing quickly moved into U.S. classrooms after the war, due in part to the popularity of Frederick Taylor's *Principles of Scientific Management* that had taken hold in public education (1911). *Scientific Management* was based on a premise that management should analyze the labor involved in manufacturing and production in order to create the greatest efficiencies in the production process.

Fast-forward almost 100 years to January 2002 and President George W. Bush's signing of the No Child Left Behind Act (NCLB; No Child Left Behind [NCLB PL 107-110], 2002). NCLB cemented annual statewide testing in mathematics and English language arts in Grades 3 through 8 and at least once in high school. Science was also to be tested once in elementary school, once in middle school, and once in high school. The results of the testing were to be used to sort students, schools, and educators into groups related to proficiency or quality.

President Barack Obama's education policy continued to rely on the use of standardized tests as a mechanism to hold school personnel accountable for student achievement. More than 40 states were awarded Race to the Top (RTTT; United States Department of Education, 2009) competitive grants or No Child Left Behind (NCLB, 2002) waivers from the U.S. Department of Education between 2010 and 2016. Each of those programs required the use of yearly student results from state standardized tests of mathematics and English language arts to rate the effectiveness of teachers, principals, and assistant principals.

The results from federally mandated, state administered tests will continue to be used by state education agencies and federal education officials to make important decisions about students, educators, and schools through 2022 as a result of the Every Child Succeeds Act signed in 2015.

The results from federally mandated, state administered tests will continue to be used by state education agencies and federal education officials to make important decisions about students, educators, and schools through 2022 as a result of the Every Child Succeeds Act signed in 2015.

Decisions, Decisions

In some states, policymakers and school leaders use the results from one test to make several different decisions. Bureaucrats in many states use the results from the state-mandated high school mathematics test to make determinations about (a) the effectiveness of the high school principal, (b) the effectiveness of the high school assistant principal(s), (c) the effectiveness of the high school math teachers, (d) whether a Grade 11 student is college ready, (e) whether that student is career ready, (f) a student's strengths and weaknesses in math as reported on standardized test student report, (g) whether the student can graduate high school, (h) whether a school is "failing," and (i) whether a school district is "failing." The "failing" status can carry with it the consequence of the school or district being closed or taken over by an education management company.

In addition, some school leaders voluntarily choose to use those same test results to (a) make judgments about the quality of the school district's mathematics program, (b) decide Grade 12 course placements for students, and (c) determine whether students must attend mandatory mathematics remedial courses. That equals 12 determinations made totally or in part from one test score. New Jersey is not an anomaly when it comes to using results from standardized tests for multiple purposes.

A dozen states used the results from the mandated high school standardized tests to determine high school graduation as of 2018, and as of the end of the 2015 school year, 40 states used the student results from standardized tests as part of their teacher evaluation systems, and 29 states used student test results as part of evaluations for school principals (Doherty & Jacobs, 2015).

In sum, it is common practice for state education policymakers and educators to use the results from a single standardized test for multiple purposes, and those purposes can carry with them important consequences for students, parents, educators, and communities at large.

Using multiple interpretations made from one test score raises issues of validity.

Using multiple interpretations made from one test score raises issues of validity.

Validity and Reliability

Test-score validity takes center stage in the debate about policies and programs that use results from standardized tests to make important decisions about educators and students. Thompson (2002) defined validity as the "degree to which scores from a measurement measure the intended construct" (p. 5). McMillan (2004) defined a construct as an "unobservable trait or characteristic such as intelligence, reading comprehension, honesty, self-concept, attitude, reasoning ability, learning style, and anxiety" (p. 63). Educators cannot measure those types of characteristics or traits directly.

The Joint Committee on Standards for Educational Evaluation (1994) stated that validity "concerns the soundness or trustworthiness of the inferences that are made from the results of the information gathering process" (p. 145). The authors of the *Standards for Educational and Psychological Testing* (AERA, APA, & NCME, 2014) defined test score validity as "the degree to which the evidence and theory support the interpretations of test scores for proposed uses of tests" (p. 11). The test result must accurately represent the construct, or characteristic being judged, in the context in which the construct is used.

For example, when a patient goes to the doctor's office for an annual check-up, the doctor might measure his height as 72 inches with a ruler attached to a scale. The number 72 signifies the height. It is appropriate for the doctor to interpret the "score" of 72 as actual height. The ruler, applied in this way, is the appropriate instrument for the construct of height and produces an output, inches, which is a valid interpretation of height. Conversely, the doctor would not interpret the results from the measurement of height as a valid indicator of the levels of LDL cholesterol in a patient. The ruler is not the appropriate instrument for the construct of LDL.

In a school context, educators should strive to ensure that (1) the test results they use to make decisions about students are derived from tests specifically designed to measure the characteristic or construct they are attempting to measure, (2) the resulting score is an accurate representation of that characteristic within the context of the measurement, and (3) the interpretations made from the results of the test accurately reflect the construct being measured.

What's Being Measured?

A test designed to measure general mathematics achievement of sixth-grade students might not be designed to determine mathematics achievement of sixth-grade students in the context of making determinations about acceptance into a gifted and talented program for mathematics.

The characteristics of a mathematically gifted sixth-grade student might not be identical to those measured by a test of general mathematics achievement. The results from a test of general Grade 6 math might not accurately represent mathematical giftedness. The results might be due to the fact that the student had parents who decided to preteach the student the content from sixth grade the summer before sixth grade. The student simply had more background knowledge and pre-exposure to the content of the test.

The authors of the *Standards for Educational and Psychological Testing* (AERA et al., 2014) provide a series of considerations regarding validity of test results for the above example:

(a) that certain skills are prerequisite for the advanced course;
(b) that the content domain of the test is consistent with these prerequisite skills; (c) that test scores can be generalized across relevant sets of items; (d) that test scores are not unduly influenced by

ancillary variables such as writing ability; (e) that success in the advanced course can be validly assessed; and (f) that test takers with high scores on the test will be more successful than test takers with low scores on the test. (p. 12)

The considerations put forth suggest that test results must satisfy several criteria for each way a test result is used in order for the score to provide valid interpretations of a construct.

Three-Legged Stool of Validity

Traditional views on validity included three parts: (1) content, (2) construct, and (3) criterion. The three parts are necessary in order to ensure that results from a measure are a valid indicator of the construct being measured. Content validity refers to the degree to which the content of the test represents the range of the content that is being tested. For example, how well does the Grade 6 mathematics test represent Grade 6 mathematics in term of topics, formats, and levels of difficulty and complexity of the entire Grade 6 math curriculum? The set of test questions must be inclusive of the entire domain of Grade 6 mathematics in order for educators to make accurate inferences about student achievement of Grade 6 mathematics.

Traditional views on validity included three parts: (1) content, (2) construct, and (3) criterion.

In the Grade 6 mathematics test example, it is important to determine whether the content of Grade 6 math is fully represented or whether the test places more emphasis on a single concept, like pre-algebra, and whether it is heavily based on reading comprehension because of text-heavy questions, instead of mathematics. Is it just a reading test with numbers?

Criterion validity describes how well the score from the test relates to an outcome. If someone wants to infer students' achievement of the entire Grade 6 math program, but the content of the test only represents a part of Grade 6 math, the results from that test would not be a valid indicator of overall Grade 6 math achievement.

Construct validity refers to how well the particular test represents the construct or trait that the test claims to measure. For instance, a clear definition of "achievement" needs to be provided in the case of the Grade 6 mathematics achievement test. What is "achievement" in the context of Grade 6 mathematics? What does "achievement" include and not include?

Does the construct of mathematics "achievement" include students being able to finish the test in a mandated period of time? Does the speed in which a student completes the test questions represent part of "achievement"? Student "achievement" could look vastly different depending on the answers to those questions.

Consequences

In addition to the traditional view of validity as three distinct categories, (1) construct, (2) content, and (3) criterion, Messick (1995) called for a view of validity that integrated criteria and content, with intended and unintended consequences within the construct validity framework. Consequential validity deals solely with the potential consequences associated with the use of the test score, not the test itself.

Consequential validity deals solely with the potential consequences associated with the use of the test score, not the test itself.

The integrated view of construct validity allows school leaders and policy makers to consider social and educational consequences in the validity discussion. Although not formally recognized as a separate type of validity, consequential validity has importance for decision making.

For example, just because a certain test produces valid results regarding Grade 6 mathematics achievement does not mean that educators should use only those results to make a determination about whether a student has learned enough of Grade 6 mathematics to be promoted to Grade 7. The unintended, evidence-based negative social and academic consequences of grade retention might outweigh the fact that the test is a valid measure of the construct of mathematics achievement. There are too many other variables that could influence the test result and obscure the student's true mathematics achievement to be used as the only decision-making data point.

Understanding consequential validity relies on school leaders' ability to realize and weigh the potential future negative consequences of the test score use against the intended outcomes. A set of research-based standards for assessment exists that can help guide educators and policymakers in regard to appropriate use of test results for decision making.

Standards of Testing

A joint committee represented by members of the American Educational Research Association (AERA), American Psychological Association (APA), and National Council on Measurement in Education (NCME) released the seventh edition of the *Standards for Educational and Psychological Testing* in 2014. The edition contains 12 categories of standards and provides specific guidance on topics that include appropriate test design, development, validity, and use of standardized tests and results (AERA et al., 2014).

Standard 1.0 provides general guidance regarding validity of results for uses related to various types of standardized testing contexts such as employment, education program placement, college entrance, and diagnostics. The standard states, "Clear articulation of each intended test score interpretation for a specified use should be set forth, and appropriate validity evidence in support of each intended interpretation should be provided" (AERA et al., 2014, p. 23).

Evidence Please

Standard 1.0 states that there needs to be evidence that the test was designed for the specific purpose for which its results are used (e.g., student placement into higher level academic math course in Grade 7) and that the results are an accurate and consistent indicator of the student performance relative to the purpose of the exam. The authors extend their warning about using test results for multiple interpretations in multiple contexts: "No test permits interpretations that are valid for all purposes or in all situations. Each recommended interpretation for a given use requires validation" (AERA et al., 2014, p. 23). Standard 1.1 further recommends, "A rationale should be presented for each intended interpretation of test scores for a given use, together with a summary of the evidence and theory bearing on the intended interpretation" (AERA et al., 2014, p. 23).

The authors of the standards present specific cautions about using results from standardized tests for multiple purposes. Standard 12.2 states, "In educational settings, when a test is designed or used to serve multiple purposes, evidence of validity, reliability/precision, and fairness should be provided for each intended use" (AERA et al., 2014, p. 195). A test designed to measure the effectiveness of a school principal may not be valid for measuring the effectiveness of a classroom teacher or college and career readiness of a student because of the differences in those constructs. The authors state clearly that one test cannot be a valid measure of multiple complex behaviors: "No one test will serve all purposes equally well" (AERA et al., 2014, p. 195).

Not Up to the Test

None of the current state assessments include validity evidence for all the ways results are interpreted and used. Determining construct validity alone would be a major task. For example, the construct of principal effectiveness is not the same as the effectiveness of the mathematics teacher or the assistant principal. Some high school assistant principals never work with instructional issues; they deal only with student discipline. Even if an assistant principal conducts classroom evaluations of teachers, it is a fool's errand to think that one 40- to 80-minute classroom evaluation and a 30-minute postobservation conference is going to influence student achievement directly.

None of the current state assessments include validity evidence for all the ways results are interpreted and used.

In addition to the locally mandated roles and responsibilities of various positions, school districts also have local teacher and school leader evaluation requirements, and many states have state professional standards and national accreditation professional standards for school administrators and teachers. Content validity would have to involve evidence that the test results from the Grade 11 mathematics test relate in some way to the various job descriptions, roles and responsibilities, evaluation requirements, and state and national accreditation standards.

Similarly, criterion validity requires that the ratings of effectiveness derived from the student results of the mathematic test relate in some way to those of perhaps the classroom evaluations, or the certification exams of the educators, or some other measures of effectiveness. One might want evidence that the ratings of effectiveness from the results of the mathematics test predict future effectives of the educators.

Student Concerns

The validity takes on additional meaning when applied to the individual student level because the decisions can change life trajectories of students. Construct and content validity play important roles in the invalid interpretations made about individual student academic strengths and weaknesses. One characteristic of tests that influences determination about skill mastery at the individual student level is the number of questions on the test.

Tests of skill mastery should include approximately 20 to 25 questions per skill in order to produce reliable results about student mastery of a specific skill (Tanner, 2001). Most of the state standardized tests in use include between three and eight questions per skill, not enough to make an accurate decision about student skill mastery at the individual level and certainly not enough to make a potentially life-altering decision about a student.

Tests of skill mastery should include approximately 20 to 25 questions per skill in order to produce reliable results about student mastery of a specific skill.

Things Might Not Be What They Seem

The authors of the *Standards for Educational and Psychological Testing* (AERA et al., 2014) caution users of test results that validity can be compromised when the test scores are influenced by ancillary variables. A pernicious set of ancillary variables includes those outside the control of educators that can predict the outcomes of standardized tests: demographic factors that relate to family human capital and community social capital.

Human capital refers to a broad set of people's skills, experiences, and abilities that allow them to potentially become more economically successful and act with greater skill (Becker, 1993; Coleman, 1988). Results from more than 50 years of research suggest that, as a group, students who live in families with more human capital have more frequent access to academically oriented life experiences that provide them with the background knowledge necessary to make more sense of school content (Scherrer, 2014).

Students with more family human capital often perform better on standardized tests of traditional academic achievement, especially those that are language arts based, because students with more life experiences tend to have larger sight and working vocabularies (Tienken, 2017). Family demographic factors such as median income, living in a single versus a two-parent household, or the percentage of female-headed families living in poverty are factors that help describe the level of human capital in a family and can be used as proxies for the human capital experienced by the student.

The community in which a student lives plays an important complimentary role in academic achievement when measured by standardized tests. Coleman (1988) explained social capital in the following way:

> Social capital is defined by its functions. It is not a single entity but a variety of different entities, with two elements in common: they all consist of some aspect of social structures, and they facilitate certain actions of actors—whether persons or corporate actors—within the structure. Like other forms of capital, social capital is productive, making possible the achievement of certain ends that in its absence would not be possible. (p. 98)

Formal and informal interactions and relationships within a community create social capital at the community level (Coleman, 1988; Flabbi & Gatti, 2018). The types of professionals that live in a community, the community groups that exist for adults, structured community recreation programs for children, religious groups, libraries, services for senior citizens and disabled residents, arts commissions, local social advocacy groups, quality and affordable daycare and preschool opportunities, and other similar resources intersect to contribute to the overall social capital of a community (Bourdieu, 1986).

Predictable Outcomes

Results from studies conducted since 1999 have demonstrated consistently that family human capital and the social capital of the community in which a child lives and matures influence the child's achievement when measured by standardized test results (e.g., Darnell, 2015; Maylone, 2002; Sackey, 2014; Wilkins, 1999).

Recent studies continue to find that standardized test results are influenced and can be predicted by family human capital and community social capital. Caldwell (2017) predicted the percentage of students who would score proficient or above on the state tests of Grade 4 mathematics and English language arts in Massachusetts. The results suggest that language arts scores could be predicted for 73% of the school districts in the sample using just two variables: percentage of families in a town with annual income less than $35,000 and the percentage of people in the community with a BA degree. Likewise, the predictions for mathematics were accurate for 74% of the school districts using only two variables: percentage of households with income over $200,000 a year and the percentage of people in a community with BA degrees.

Tienken et al. (2017) conducted a three-year longitudinal study that predicted test results in Grades 6 through 8 for the New Jersey state-mandated standardized tests in mathematics and English language arts for 70% and 78% of the schools in the samples. Their samples ranged from 292 to 311 public schools that serviced Grades 6 through 8 in New Jersey. The results suggested that, in most cases, the variables of (a) percentage of families in a community with income over $200,000 a year, (b) percentage of people in a community in poverty, and (c) percentage of people in a community with bachelor's degrees were able to predict the percentage of students in Grades 6, 7, and 8 in each school who would score proficient or above on the New Jersey standardized tests.

Ecological Systems Theory

Ecological Systems Theory provides a framework from which educators can understand the phenomenon and overcome it. Bronfenbrenner (1979) posited that children exist in an ecological system, and various layers of the system exert influence upon them. Family, school, peer groups, and community intersect to directly and indirectly influence behaviors and outcomes of children. A combination of family human capital and community social capital factors can predict student test results at the school level because the school is within the ecological system of children and is thus influenced by the other factors within the system.

Ecological systems theory comports with research-based perspectives of poverty that suggest the importance of providing children the formal education resources necessary for learning at high levels and ensuring that appropriate social supports are in place so that children can make full use of the resources they encounter in formal learning environments. Known as the *capabilities perspective*, the line of research suggests students can have varying capabilities to use and transform educational resources into concrete learning gains (Scherrer, 2014, p. 203).

One way to gain an accurate understanding of a child is by considering the various layers of the system in which a child lives and is raised. The capabilities perspective is another layer within the ecological system that influences learning, and it should be considered when interpreting standardized test results.

So What? Understanding the Big Picture of Assessment Use

This section provides leaders with an example critique of test use and abuse as viewed through the reflective questions from the six lenses of the critique framework.

1. How well does the use of standardized test results to make important interpretations about students and educators forward the historical democratic aims of public education?

The interpretations about students and educators made from standardized test results might not be accurate unless the test results have been validated for each type of interpretation made. It is ill advised to make a decision that can alter a student's educational trajectory in a direction of less access, less opportunity, or less equity based on one test score. As of 2019, none of the test results obtained from the tests currently used to satisfy the ESSA of 2015 requirements for state testing have been validated for all the interpretations made from their results.

The purpose of education is narrowed to a myopic view of what it means to be economically viable in the workforce. The economic purpose becomes the focus when test results are interpreted for high-stakes purposes without being validated. Educators should be wary of multiple interpretations

Figure 5.1 • Six Lenses of Critique

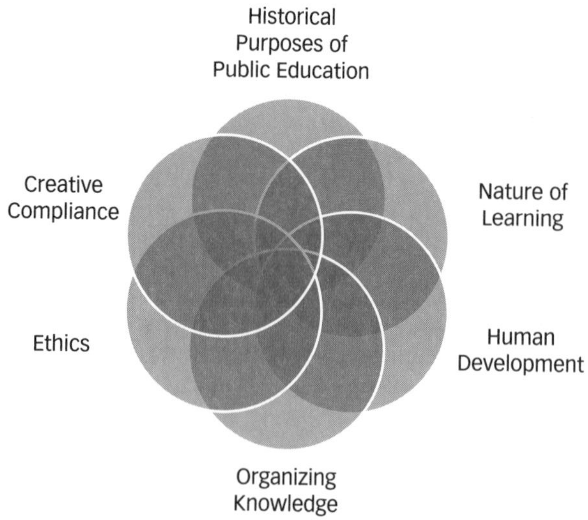

Historical Purposes of Public Education

Creative Compliance

Nature of Learning

Ethics

Human Development

Organizing Knowledge

made from test results that come from the same test. The invalid use of test results represents education malpractice. The tests simply do not assess the full breadth of the written curricula nor do they address sociocivic or avocational aims (Koretz, 2009).

The invalid use of test results represents education malpractice.

Dewey (1929) warned more broadly that quantitative results do not tell the entire story about students' academic potential or sociocivic and avocational dispositions. Multiple measures must be used that address the totality of public schooling purposes, based on curricula that reflect the various aims:

> Exact quantitative determinations are far from meeting the demands of such situations, for they presuppose repetitions and exact uniformities. Exaggeration of their importance tends to cramp judgment, to substitute uniform rules for free play of thought, and to emphasize the mechanical factors that also exist in schools . . . they do not give any help in larger questions of reconstruction of curriculum and methods. (pp. 65–66)

2. How well does the use of standardized testing allow the organization and delivery of knowledge to be customized to maximize active learning and participation of the target audience?

Results from studies on the topic suggest that curricula are narrowed in scope and become more discipline centered and less student centered when high stakes are attached to standardized test results (Berliner, 2011; Holcombe, Jennings, & Koretz, 2013; Koretz, 2017). Educators also narrow their instructional methods to those in which transmission of information takes precedence over teaching students how to learn, and the scope of instruction is often narrowed to the formats most likely to appear on the tests (Au, 2011; Jones, 2008).

3. What are the implications of the reform for those inside and outside the range of the developmental stage upon which the reform rests?

The use of standardized test results to make high-stakes decisions about what students know and can do by the end of a grade level is based on a fixed view of learning in which all students are expected to know the same content and demonstrate the same skills, in the same format, on the same day. The fixed view of student achievement is at odds with the research that demonstrates cognitive, social, and emotional development occurs in stages, and there can be large variance in the time span when students master a specific stage of development. Just because a student cannot master a topic today does not mean the student will not master the topic in the future, and just because the student demonstrated mastery of a topic on a standardized test does not mean the student actually learned anything. The student could have already come to school with the topic mastered due to the student's family and community capital.

4. How well does the reform acknowledge the target audience (e.g., student, teacher) as an active constructor of meaning who brings prior knowledge to the situation?

Students are often placed in the role of passive receiver of knowledge as teachers try to prepare students for traditional standardized tests. Following the release of the results, students are subjected to instructional interventions, in the name of improving perceived deficiencies supposedly identified by tests that have not been validated to identify individual student strengths and weaknesses (Madaus, Russell, & Higgins, 2009). School leaders should resist the urge to make important decisions about students and teachers based upon the results from standardized tests.

Ethical Considerations

5. How does the reform impact the recognition and respect of stakeholders' dignity as human beings and the right to exhibit unique characteristics and behaviors, and what can I do about it?

The use of scores from standardized tests as the deciding factor to make important decisions about students and educators can result in students and educators being labeled in some of same ways people label inanimate objects. Partially proficient, basic skills, Title I, at risk, bubble kid, struggling student, not effective, and a plethora of other terms that education reformers use can cause the dehumanization of educators and students. After students and educators are no longer viewed as human it becomes easier to enact policies and programs that negatively affect them, policies and programs that often lack evidence.

The erosion of human dignity can lead to using mechanistic education methods such as keeping students from attending recess or cocurricular opportunities in favor of computer test preparation courses, declaring students as young as 9 or 10 not college or career ready, zero tolerance policies, limiting access to quality curriculum, and labeling teachers and schools as failing.

Educators must work to defend the human dignity of students and their peers and reject the urge and practice of labeling based on standardized test results that can be easily predicted by factors outside the control of schools.

Educators must work to defend the human dignity of students and their peers and reject the urge and practice of labeling based on standardized test results that can be easily predicted by factors outside the control of schools.

Creative Compliance: Now What?

1. What creative compliance strategies can I take, within my sphere of influence, that will help to revise the education reform or capitalize upon it to become more aligned with the Curriculum Paradigm and the ethics of justice and care, in order to do less harm and more good?

Tacking

Although some state education agencies and school leaders mandate that educators identify students as gifted and talented, special needs, basic skills, or the myriad other labels used in schools based on standardized test results, individual school leaders can work with their staff to see beyond the labels and view students as unique human beings. School leaders can tack away from labeling and simply state that all students have value and that educators must work to discover that value and make it visible to all.

Egalitarianism and dignity are ideas, like democracy, and like democracy, egalitarianism and dignity must be defended and nurtured by leadership actions at the local level in order to cultivate and preserve them. School leaders can lead by example and not label students or educators in ways that dehumanize them based on test scores. They can overtly correct those who label students and educators and apply ethics of justice and the importance of the relationship between an egalitarian public school system and a healthy democracy.

School is the primary venue in which students become socialized to an egalitarian and democratic community life. It is a place where they learn how their individual actions impact others and the greater good. If leaders covertly, or overtly, label students and other educators, or allow the practice of labeling to occur, then some human beings will be deemed as more worthy of dignity than others based on a test score. Those individuals will then learn to devalue egalitarian principles in favor of principles aligned with a quantitative meritocracy in which human dignity is reduced to a number.

The historic purposes of public education require school leaders take a stand toward more egalitarian practices. How can leaders claim to be committed to developing all students to their potential on one hand and then sort them into groups who receive a more enriched education and those who receive a more mechanistic, test-prep driven education on the other hand? Leaders must seize the opportunity to be a compliance entrepreneur and tack away from inhuman labeling and move toward a more egalitarian approach in which all students and educators are referred to in ways that acknowledge their human dignity.

The historic purposes of public education require school leaders take a stand toward more egalitarian practices.

Circumventing

School leaders can circumvent bad practice by banning the voluntary use of standardized test results to make important decisions about students and educators if they have the authority within their sphere of influence to do so. School leaders can also work with teaching staff to de-emphasize the importance of the results from standardized tests by fostering the use of multiple data points, based on actual classroom student performance over time, to make decisions.

School leaders can partially circumvent a system that uses standardized test results as the deciding factor for student selection into academic programs by creating an internal secondary system based on multiple measures. Teachers can recommend students for secondary review who did not qualify for quality academic programs due to test scores or those who are placed in low-level remedial programs. A school leader could use multiple measures from the secondary system to either unilaterally place the student into a program or to negotiate with a supervisor to change the student placement.

School leaders can partially circumvent a system that uses standardized test results as the deciding factor for student selection into academic programs by creating an internal secondary system based on multiple measures.

Negotiating

The Wildwood School District in Wildwood, New Jersey, provides an example of school leaders who have developed an internal system of multiple measures for decision making about student learning and teaching and then used that system to negotiate changes in district policy. The system has been in use since the 2010–2011 school year.

For example, three classroom-based data points are used to make decisions about student learning and teaching effectiveness in English language arts: (1) student reading levels derived from running records conferences with students three times a year—autumn, winter, and later spring, (2) classroom assessments of literal and inferential comprehension that occur through the year, and (3) schoolwide writing prompts administered three times a year, like the reading level assessments, and scored by groups of teachers and an independent writing coach. Secondary measures include classroom activities and a commercial assessment of phonemic and phonetic awareness in the primary grades.

The frequency of the assessments coupled with their proximity to the student makes the results more valid as indicators of student performance than a one-time, commercial standardized test that is developed distally from the students and context of Wildwood, New Jersey. The data derived from the assessments have proven to be accurate indicators of student performance and effective teaching practices.

The system was a result of negotiations between the principal and former superintendent as part of an overall program to provide more equitable and effective education to the students of Wildwood. The principal made evidence-based arguments and provided concrete details about the development and implementation of the system, advantages of the system compared to the previous practice of using standardized test results, and the overall benefits to teachers and students.

CHAPTER 5

School leaders who find themselves in a situation in which they are mandated to use test results to make high-stakes decisions regarding things like entrance into programs such as gifted and talented and basic skills can attempt to negotiate the use of multiple methods to compliment the standardized test results based on the three-legged stool approach. The Wildwood system of multiple measures can be a good example of such a system during negotiations.

Try This!

- What are some examples in which standardized test results might be misused in your setting, and what can you do about it?

- What ethical dilemmas are created?

- Which creative compliance strategies can you use, and why?

- What opportunities exist to capitalize on testing or redefine it so that it increases educational opportunities and quality for all students?

- What potential problems do you foresee, and what can you do about them now and for a Plan B?

Leadership Take-Away: Testing Use

A multiple-measures approach to assessment can yield a more complete picture of students' cognitive, social-emotional, and physical development and increase the chances that any interpretations made could be more valid representations of the construct being measured.

Leader Quick Tip

Use of Test Results

Use at least three data points, from different types of measurements, when making important decisions about students or teachers. Maintain an egalitarian culture, and do not label and dehumanize people based on test results.

Next Steps

School leaders have the ability to influence the use of test results as decision-making tools. They can choose the interpretations they make or whether they use the results at all. A multiple-measures approach to assessment can yield a more complete picture of students' cognitive, social-emotional, and physical development and increase the chances that any interpretations made could be more valid representations of the construct being measured.

Teacher effectiveness is another construct that policymakers in many states are tying to student standardized test results. The next chapter provides a critique of teacher merit pay based on standardized test results and creative compliance ideas that school leaders can use to help blunt the force of merit pay policies when they deem them educationally unsound.

Chapter 6

CASE STUDY 3
Merit Pay

The case provides an example critique of merit pay in education settings and presents creative compliance examples for educators who must implement merit pay. Pay for performance systems, or merit pay as it is often called, based on results from students' state mandated standardized tests, is a policy idea that continues to gain traction in the halls of the U.S. Congress and state legislatures. Defined in the literature as an "individual-based annual bonus," merit pay is often operationalized in education as a one-time event that does not increase the regular salary of the recipient (Park & Sturman, 2012).

Since 2002, an increasing number of states included student standardized test results as part of the teacher evaluation rating system. As of the start of the 2016 school year, 40 states used results from standardized tests as part of their teacher evaluation systems, and 29 states used student test results as part of evaluations for school principals (Doherty & Jacobs, 2015).

Money for Merit

The George W. Bush presidential administration created the federal Teacher Incentive Fund (TIF) in 2006 to encourage states to institute merit pay for educators. The Bush administration set the initial funding at $99 million, and that funding increased under President Obama to over $435 million through proposals embedded in the Race to the Top competitive grant program and other funding mechanisms (Marsh, 2012).

The Race to the Top (RTTT) federal grant program required states to link the evaluations and pay of school administrators and teachers to student performance. States such as Colorado, Texas, New Jersey, Missouri, Florida, Tennessee, Nevada, Idaho, Illinois, Indiana, and others passed legislation or have bills under consideration to link administrator or teacher pay to student performance measured in part or totally by results on summative state-mandated standardized tests of academic skills and knowledge.

Theoretical Frameworks for Merit Pay

Expectancy Theory and Process Theory support many of the large merit pay programs implemented in the United States. Expectancy Theory proposes that a person makes rational decisions about how hard to work based on (a) an expectation that the effort will lead to a personally satisfying outcome and (b) how much the person values the intended outcome. Supporters of merit pay based on student test results assume that teachers will work harder and produce better standardized test scores in exchange for a monetary reward.

Supporters of merit pay based on student test results assume that teachers will work harder and produce better standardized test scores in exchange for a monetary reward.

The Porter-Lawler model, rooted in Process Theory, is the foundation upon which Expectancy Theory is operationalized (Porter & Lawler, 1968). The Porter-Lawler model substantiates the use of external stimulus, merit pay reward, to entice people to do more work or put more effort into the predetermined goals related to the merit pay. Most of the large-scale experiments with merit pay for teachers in the United States focus on a one-time bonus for teachers who produce higher student test scores.

The goal of higher test scores is set by an external entity, not the teachers or school leaders. All of the large-scale merit pay programs attempted in the United States are based in some way on the Porter-Lawler model in which the goals and stimuli are externally set and the teachers and school leaders are directed to meet the goals and accept the stimuli.

Behaviorism

The behaviorist theory of operant conditioning (Skinner, 1938, 1953) connects to the Porter-Lawler model in that the stimuli used to change teacher behavior focus on a narrow organizational goal: increasing standardized test scores. Operant conditioning describes processes used to modify behaviors based on positive and negative reinforcement, the centerpiece of the Porter-Lawler model. Operant conditioning is most common in merit pay programs that rely on one-time rewards for teachers.

In the case of merit pay, teachers adjust their teaching to achieve the external objectives set by policymakers or school administrators. If the merit pay reward is based on student standardized test scores, it is theorized that teachers will teach more of the content most likely to be on the standardized test and spend more time preparing students for the test in order to receive the reward.

Stimulus-Response

Operant conditioning is a form of stimulus-response psychology. Stimulus-response psychology is the "science for controlling others" (Bredo, 2002, p. 25). It is also based on the premise that punishment and lack of punishment will motivate people to achieve the goals set for them (Rescorla & Wagner, 1972). Merit pay, or lack of merit pay, acts as the reward and punishment stimuli. Operant conditioning is rooted in experimental work with animals and controlling the behavior of animals (Skinner, 1938, 1953).

Lazy Educators

McGregor's (1960) Theory X is another theory that explains why some policymakers enact merit pay programs. Theory X gives insight into the reason some merit pay proposals are created: The bias of some policymakers is that educators are lazy. Merit pay evaluation systems are created in part to force educators to work harder toward externally set goals because there is an underlying assumption that educators are lazy and they will work harder for more money.

The bias of some policymakers is that educators are lazy.

Yet, in some merit pay systems, the educators feel as if they cannot succeed because they view the system as subjective, unfairly structured, or they know that out-of-school factors such as family capital and community capital influence standardized test scores (Tienken, 2016). Thus, Reactance Theory (Brehm, 1972) is a part of every merit pay system as evidenced by the ways in which some teachers withdraw from active participation in the school, try to subvert the merit pay system by cheating on standardized tests, lose morale, decrease overall instructional efficacy, or stop collaborating with their colleagues.

Previous Experience With Merit Pay in Education

There exist results from studies of large merit pay programs in places such as New York City; Nashville, Tennessee; Round Rock, Texas; Austin, Texas; Newark, New Jersey; and the Teacher Advancement Program (TAP) that operated in 15 states (e.g., Fryer, 2011; Marsh, 2012; Springer, Ballou, & Peng, 2008; Springer et al., 2009; Springer, Ballou et al., 2012; Springer, Pane et al., 2012). Statewide merit pay programs based on the results from student standardized tests have also been implemented in towns and cities in Colorado, Florida, Michigan, Minnesota, South Carolina, and in Washington, DC.

In almost all cases, the merit pay programs based on standardized test results had no statistically significant effects on student achievement as measured by standardized tests or very small overall effect sizes, less than 0.15, not worth the time or money spent. Yet, hundreds of millions of dollars and countless hours of teacher time were spent on the initiatives.

In almost all cases, the merit pay programs based on standardized test results had no statistically significant effects on student achievement as measured by standardized tests or very small overall effect sizes, less than 0.15, not worth the time or money spent.

Whether the merit pay was awarded on an individual basis, like the programs in Nashville, Tennessee, or on a team basis like in Round Rock, Texas, or on a schoolwide basis, like in New York City, the results were not statistically relevant, and many resources were devoted to the effort that might have been used for better purposes. New York City spent $75 million on its school-based merit pay program during a three-year experiment from 2007 to 2010 and found no statistically significant increase in student test results in mathematics and language arts (Fryer, 2011).

Entire schools in New York City were eligible for the merit pay if standardized tests scores in the schools increased. The idea was to use merit pay to unite the teaching in entire schools around the goal of increasing standardized test results. The $75 million spent on the program could have been used to lift almost 8,000 families in New York City out of poverty for at least one year and provided additional life opportunities to the children of those families.

There had not been any large-scale empirical studies of the influence of merit pay on student four-year public school high school graduation and the dropout rate, on a national scale, until 2012. Guis (2012) conducted a national study, using district-level 2007–2008 data from the School and Staffing Survey (SASS). The sample included over 1,600 school districts. The findings suggested that merit pay did not have a significant influence on average graduation rates and dropout rates.

There are documented negative effects on the overall education experiences that students receive when their teachers are part of merit pay programs based on tests results. Au (2011) reported his findings from a meta-analysis that an important reaction to standardization, including teacher evaluation based on student test scores, was the narrowing of the curriculum to the topics most likely tested and teaching the curriculum in the format mostly likely used on the tests. Instead of improving and enriching the education experiences for students, merit pay appears to restrict and impoverish education experiences.

Profit Over People

Merit pay is most commonly used in the for-profit jobs that evaluate employees on some type of clearly quantifiable output such as sales and manufacturing that includes timed work, like assembling consumer electronics. Merit pay is also used in some human services professions such as nursing, but the merit is based on accomplishing tasks that are easily quantified and short term in nature and not based on client outcomes, like responding to a patient call bell within a stipulated time period (Glassman, Glassman, Champagne, & Zugelder, 2010).

The nurse is not judged on how well the patient responds to the medical intervention that takes place after the nurse answers the call bell, whereas merit pay proposals for public schools judge the teacher on how well the student responds to the instructional intervention.

Increasing company profits is a motivating factor for the implementation of merit pay systems as evidenced by the more frequent use of such systems in the for-profit business sector compared to the nonprofit sector. The for-profit sector has different desires and interests related to evaluation of employee output compared to the nonprofit sector. For-profit businesses are focused on making money.

Students are human beings, not part of a profit margin. Teachers work to develop the whole child in terms of sociocivic orientations and avocational aspects, not only academically. The aims of teaching and child development seem at odds with the for-profit business assumptions that underlie merit pay.

Students are human beings, not part of a profit margin.

Why Teachers Choose to Teach

Herzberg's Two-Factory Theory of Motivation helps explain some potential negative effects that can occur with teacher merit pay based on student standardized test results (Herzberg, 1966; Herzberg, Mausner, & Snyderman, 1959). Although Herzberg and colleagues originally conducted research with accountants and engineers in Pittsburgh, Pennsylvania, the basic ideas of Herzberg's Theory apply to teachers in public school settings in the United States and other countries.

Herzberg theorized that internal factors related to a person's work, like more autonomy over planning, implementing, and evaluating work, help to motivate the person and increase job satisfaction. Encouraging creativity, risk taking, and innovation by employees through more autonomy over their work leads to more productivity, more creativity, higher levels of quality, and overall satisfaction with work.

Factors like pay do not increase motivation. Pay can decrease motivation when pay is not comparable to similar jobs; however, employees will not become more motivated by more pay, but they will become disenfranchised by low pay. Employees are motivated by the quality of the work.

Results from surveys of why teachers choose the teaching profession suggest that it is the intrinsic value of the work of teaching that is the motivating factor, whereas salary is an extrinsic factor and does not motivate teachers to work any harder (Webb et al., 2004). Although pay is necessary, more pay does not necessarily generate greater job satisfaction or teacher output as measured by student test results.

Results from Tienken (2009) and other studies published in a book by Sandra Chistolini (2009) from the University of Roma Tre, in Rome, Italy, align with Herzberg's Two-Factor Theory of Motivation. Teachers from Italy, the United States, Poland, Belgium, Cyprus, Libya, Slovakia, and Turkey responded that they chose the teaching profession because they find the work meaningful and they believe they make a difference in the world. Teachers indicated they were intrinsically motivated by their work with students, the social value of the profession, and opportunities for personal growth, not by an external monetary reward (Chistolini, 2009). Teachers in the study indicated that they were committed to professionalism and helping students to mature cognitively and emotionally, not economic stimuli.

Self-Determination

The reasons given by teachers as to why they choose teaching align more with Self-Determination Theory (Ryan & Deci, 2000) than with Stimulus-Response Theory or Process Theory. Self-Determination Theory suggests that people have three main psychological needs that must be met in order to produce intrinsic motivation. People grow more professionally and personally when the needs are met. The three needs are (1) competence, (2) relatedness, and (3) autonomy. In the education setting, the needs relate to (a) professional competence, (b) collegiality, and (c) professional autonomy.

Mulder (2014) defined professional competence as a set of knowledge, skills, dispositions, and attitudes necessary to perform effectively according to professional and ethical standards. Collegiality is represented by teachers cooperating to enhance their effectiveness with students. Cooperation can take the form of collaborating on pedagogical projects, sharing resources, working together in professional learning communities, or other forms of authentic teamwork (Shah, 2016), as is often practiced in modern medicine.

Dewey (1924) equated professional autonomy with teacher emancipation and linked student creativity and autonomy to the professional autonomy of teachers. He warned that one could not expect student creativity and independent learning without professional autonomy for teachers:

> Finally, I saw how inconsistent it was to expect this greater amount of creative, independent work from the student when the teachers are still unemancipated; when the teachers were still shackled by too many rules and prescriptions and too much of a desire for uniformity of method and subject matter. (p. 470)

So What? Understanding the Big Picture of Merit Pay

This section provides leaders with an example critique of merit pay as viewed through the reflective questions from four of the six lenses of the critique framework.

Figure 6.1 • **Four Lenses of Critique**

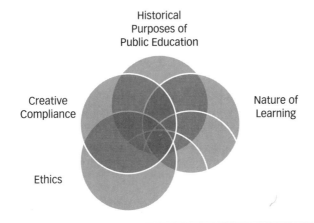

1. How well does the proposal place the target audience (e.g., teacher) in the role of active constructor of meaning who brings prior knowledge to the situation?

Merit pay based on student results from standardized tests places the teacher in the role of the passive implementer or test preparation technician. The student often must assume the role of passive receiver of information and imitator of processes because standardized test questions most often allow for just one predetermined answer, not original thinking. The overt message of merit pay programs based on standardized test results is to raise student test scores using any methods necessary.

The overt message of merit pay programs based on standardized test results is to raise student test scores using any methods necessary.

---

2. How well does merit pay based on standardized test results forward the historical democratic aims of public education?

The sociocivic function of public education is one that seems to be overlooked by the proponents of merit pay based on standardized test results. Dewey (1929) explained the sociocivic role of public education in nurturing a democracy:

> For the creation of a democratic society we need an educational system where the process of moral intellectual development is in practice as well as in theory a cooperative transaction of inquiry engaged in by free, independent human beings who treat ideas and the heritage of the past as means and methods for the further enrichment of life, quantitatively and qualitatively, who use the good attained for the discovery and establishment of something better. (p. 84)

Merit pay based on standardized test results ignores the sociocivic and avocational aims of education and focuses only on a narrow interpretation of the economic aim.

Ethical Considerations

3. How is the greater good of students or educators in the local education community marginalized or enhanced by implementing the reform?

On its face, merit pay makes practical sense and aligns with the ethics of justice and care; reward educators who produce better academic results with students, and that is an overall good thing for students. However, higher student scores on standardized tests might not be indicative of actual student learning, and the goal of producing better results can result in practices that are not educative and actually do harm.

The negative effects of merit pay can be attributed to the phenomenon identified by Campbell (1976) as the "corrupting effect of quantitative indicators" (p. 49), also known as Campbell's Law. The law states, "the more any quantitative social indicator is used for social decision-making, the more subject it will be to corruption pressures and the more apt it will be to distort and corrupt the social processes it is intended to monitor" (Campbell, 1979, p. 85).

The high-profile cheating scandals reported in the mainstream media that occurred in Atlanta, Washington, DC, Philadelphia, Chicago, and New York City between 2003 and 2013 aptly demonstrate the corrupting effects of merit pay based on standardized test scores on the education process

(Kirp, 2013). Each example of high-stakes cheating included instances of educators providing students with answers, teachers changing answers on student answer sheets, or teachers transforming classroom instruction into nothing more than test preparation sessions.

Campbell (1976) seemingly predicted those scandals some 35 years earlier when he wrote, "when test scores become the goal of the teaching process, they both lose their value as indicators of educational status and distort the educational process in undesirable ways" (p. 52). Campbell documented instances in which educators administered the pretests in confusing ways that produced lower scores and then provided more assistance on the posttest and produced higher scores to receive rewards.

Prior to Campbell's prediction, Stake (1971) documented a large-scale test-score cheating incident that occurred during the Texarkana Performance Contracting experiment. Private contractors were paid to provide supplemental instructional services to students who were deemed as undereducated based on results from standardized tests. The program was similar to the supplementary educational services (SES) contracting program later implemented during No Child Left Behind (NCLB) and the Every Student Succeeds Act (ESSA) program of *Pay for Success*.

The NCLB SES program required schools with low student standardized test scores to use part of their federal Title I basic skills monies to pay outside education contractors to provide supplemental education tutoring after school in an effort to raise test scores. Similarly, the 2015 ESSA Pay for Performance program provides federal monies to organizations that provide interventions that raise standardized test results. The potential corrupting effects of such programs are readily apparent because similar programs in the past created similar issues. These circumstances beg the following ethical question:

1. How does the reform impact the recognition and respect of stakeholders' dignity as human beings and the right to exhibit unique characteristics and behaviors?

Although some educators might think they are upholding an ethic of care by helping students produce higher standardized test results, the opposite can be true if they are using means that are counterproductive, like narrowing curriculum and large doses of test preparation. The corrupting effects of merit pay can destroy the human relationship between educator and student over time and undermine public trust in the profession and education system.

Educators begin to view students as an inanimate test score and a profit center, when combined with merit pay, and not as a unique human being with individual interests and passions worthy of being developed academically and socially. Likewise, when educators apply test preparation strategies, they narrow the curriculum to content that is most likely tested in formats that will most likely appear on the test (Au, 2011). Test preparation invalidates standardized test results because it is impossible to determine if the students actually learned anything or if they are simply imitating processes and regurgitating facts most likely tested (Koretz, 2009).

The ethic of justice is perverted by the corruption of education processes when monetary value is placed on test results. The individual with the power, the teacher or school leader, uses that power to implement educationally bankrupt practices for personal gain at the expense of the student. The educator puts his or her individual needs above those of others and the larger educational community, and in the process, breaks the social contract between public education and the student, and the public at large, because effective education ceases when corrupt processes are used.

Creative Compliance: Now What?

Merit pay programs are most commonly mandated at the state level, and the regulations do not allow school administrators to deviate from the basic structure of how teachers are rated. A common structure for merit pay schemes is to use a combination of student standardized test results and classroom observation ratings to arrive at a summative numerical rating for a teacher. Most evaluation schemes use a rating scale of 1 to 4 and set a cut-score for proficient teaching and merit pay. In some states, the score is set at a 2.65 to be deemed a proficient teacher, whereas in others it is a 2.75. In some states, a 3.5 or higher is necessary to receive the best ranking and merit pay.

Some state evaluation systems derive the final evaluation score from a 50% weighting of standardized test results and 50% weighting from one to three classroom observations. Some states allow for a third or fourth indicator of academic achievement, sometimes dictated by the state and sometimes chosen by the school district.

The summative score is determined based on the indicators, but the mathematical weight of each indicator does not have to be distributed evenly. A state can choose to use a 50% weight on standardized test results, 30% on classroom observations, and 20% on the other academic indicator. The school administrator rarely controls all of the indicators or how the teacher rating is computed.

1. What creative compliance strategies can I use to slow or blunt the education reform, if necessary, so as to create space from which to change the proposal to become more aligned with the Curriculum Paradigm and the ethics of justice and care at the point of contact with students or educators?

Cracking the Code

State-mandated merit pay policies do not provide a lot of room for customization at the school level. With that said, there exist cracks in the system that provide opportunities for change if the school leader knows where to look. Cracking the code is the first and most important creative compliance strategy to use in the case of merit pay programs. The school leader must clearly understand the teacher evaluation merit pay scheme being used in order to select the appropriate creative compliance strategies.

Cracking the code is the first and most important creative compliance strategy to use in the case of merit pay programs.

The school leader must read the actual state code and/or school district policy associated with the teacher evaluation scheme. The mathematical algorithm for the final evaluation rating is usually embedded in the state code or a school district policy. The algorithm forms the basis from which to find cracks for creative compliance.

For example, one state used a three-part evaluation system that included 30% based on standardized test results, 50% based on classroom observation ratings, and 20% based on two academic achievement objectives developed by individual teachers and required teachers to achieve a summative score of 2.65 out of a possible 4 points to be considered effective. Earning below a 2.65 resulted in a teacher being put on a corrective action plan for the school year.

School leaders who understood the mathematics behind the scheme were able to show their teachers that as long as they performed well on their classroom observation, which the school administrator influenced, and their individual academic objectives, they could actually receive the lowest possible score on their standardized testing portion and still be rated effective. Showing the teachers the mathematics behind the system helped to alleviate fear and removed some of the pressure to focus on test preparation or cheat on standardized tests.

A teacher who scored an average of a 3.0 on classroom observations, a 3.5 on the individually developed academic objective, and a 1.5 (almost the lowest rating possible) on the standardized testing still managed to be rated a 2.65, and was considered proficient in that state. The mathematics is straightforward: $(3.0 \times 0.5) + (3.5 \times 0.2) + (1.5 \times 0.3) = 2.65$.

Teachers need to understand that depending on the formula and the measures used, their jobs might not be on the line, and thus, they can focus on good teaching, because it is good teaching that will produce the best results for them and their students in the long term. School leaders who hype the evaluation scheme in an attempt to scare or motivate teachers might actually be engaging in unethical behavior and education malpractice if that hyping causes educationally bankrupt practices to be carried out with students.

School leaders should make a point to tell their faculty their positions on unethical teaching and setting expectations for not devolving education into test preparation, not purchasing test preparation materials, disavowing merit pay, and supporting teachers with professional development for evidence-informed teaching practices can help improve classroom teaching and reduce the corrupting influence of merit pay.

It is true that in some states in which the standardized test score is worth 50% or more of the teachers' evaluation scores it might be impossible to fully overcome the system. However, reducing oneself to an accomplice in a bureaucratically mandated system that is rigged against educators does not provide school leaders a free pass to engage in educational malpractice by supporting narrow curricula, engaging in test preparation instead of evidence-informed instruction, or pressuring students for test results. School leaders can decide to coach teachers on quality instruction and award them high classroom observation scores instead.

Negotiating, Piloting, and Waivers

The leader could engage in a combination of negotiation, piloting, and a waiver if the school district has some control over the contours of the system. Even if the school district has no control over the mandated system, a school leader can negotiate a parallel system based on evidence, like was done in Wildwood with the assessment system noted in Chapter 5.

Local teaching evaluation committees can develop local criteria and evidence rubrics based on factors that teachers and school personnel have more control over rather than students' results on standardized exams: (a) the quality of opportunities teachers and other school personnel create, design, and implement for students to experience the three historic functions of public school; (b) the types of opportunities teachers create and implement for students to follow their passions and interests and express their creativity and innovativeness; (c) how teachers organize and customize the curriculum so that students are able to be active participators in their education; (d) the ways in which teachers build rapport with their students; (e) the types of opportunities teachers and other school personnel create for students to become lifelong learners; and (f) the opportunities teachers and other school personnel provide students to explore entrepreneurial interests within the context of socially conscious problem solving.

Local customization can also occur through opportunities for teachers and school leaders to add criteria related to local school goals that could then be used to evaluate the entire school. The local faculty of teachers could decide those factors and require a majority of the staff to achieve consensus on the criteria.

A parallel system based on the examples presented above relates more to the motivations of teachers while also aligning to the general functions of public school in a democratic society and how students learn. They align to self-determination theory and Herzberg's Two-Factor Theory of Motivation and include teachers in the development of the evaluation system.

Try This!

- What are some examples in which merit of any sort is used in your setting, and what can you do about it?

- What ethical dilemmas are created?

- Which creative compliance strategies can you use, and why?

- What opportunities exist to capitalize on the program or redefine it so that it increases educational opportunities and quality for all students?

- What potential problems do you foresee, and what can you do about them now and for a Plan B?

Leadership Take-Away: Merit Pay

Read the code and regulations in search of any cracks from which to creatively comply. Understand the algorithm used to calculate the merit and attempt to influence or control the inputs into that algorithm to lessen the negative effects on students and teachers and leverage any positive aspects.

Read the code and regulations in search of any cracks from which to creatively comply.

Next Steps

Educators need to move beyond the noise and corporate marketing of pay-for-performance schemes based on student test results and educate themselves on recent empirical evidence on the subject. Very few white-collar private sector professionals receive performance pay based on a single or very narrow set of indicators. Only 6% of private sector employees received direct, output-based cash payments according to the 2005 National Compensation Survey (Adams, Heywood, & Rothstein, 2009; Springer, Ballou et al., 2012; Springer, Pane et al., 2012). Most of those workers were in commission-based fields like used-car sales, penny-stock brokers, and real estate agents; hardly comparable professions to that of raising children to be productive, ethical, and moral citizens.

As Dewey (1924) stated, how can students learn to actively participate in a democracy, critique ideas, and think creatively, complexly, and innovatively if their teachers are prisoners of a standardized system aimed at fostering conformity and ruled by autocratic forces. Therefore, any teaching evaluation system needs to be nonconformist in nature but based on a common paradigm developed from the historical purposes of schooling, research, theories on how students learn best, and the motivating factors for teachers.

Any system of evaluation must free teachers to create and innovate, not constrain them. It must provide clear criteria, customized to the specific situation of the school, so that they have opportunities to demonstrate their accomplishments in ways that are transparent, democratic, and child centered.

Part III

PROMISING PRACTICES

Chapter 7

CASE STUDY 4
Recess of the Mind

Walking in Their Shoes

This case presents a critique of the promising practice of *Recess of the Mind* to increase overall student well-being and provides school leaders with strategies to capitalize on general mindfulness techniques in schools.

If you ever followed a student around for a day you might have been surprised to find how much time is spent passively sitting and listening. There seems to be a premium placed upon sitting up straight, facing forward, and attending to the teacher. I used to give those exact instructions to my elementary school students (I apologize, class! You were great despite my teaching!). Considering that students can spend more than 350 minutes a day in formal instructional settings, the amount of time spent sitting up, facing forward, and attending to the teacher could seem overwhelming to most students.

If you ever followed a student around for day you might have been surprised to find how much time is spent passively sitting and listening.

It is overwhelming because it is abnormal. Children aren't wired to sit. Yet, many aspects of standardized curricula, standardized tests, and technology-based skill and drill activities that students encounter on a daily basis require stamina, or the ability to keep working for extended amounts of time without real movement or a mental break.

When I was a public school assistant superintendent for curriculum and instruction I used to follow students' class schedules a few times a year. I followed students with different types of schedules. I followed students eligible for basic skills, students in advanced courses, student athletes, and so on, to get a sense of what types of learning experiences different types of students received. It was a test of endurance on some days. On other days, it was invigorating.

Move It, Recess!

The American Academy of Pediatrics (2013) stated that "Recess is a necessary break in the day for optimizing a child's social, emotional, physical, and cognitive development. In essence, recess should be considered a child's personal time." The American Academy of Pediatrics categorized an effective recess as "one where children demonstrate their ability to stay within the boundaries of their play space, negotiate conflict with each other, and then return to academic learning."

Pasi Sahlberg (2018) explained the importance and impact of recess on Finnish students in his book *FinnishEd Leadership*. Sahlberg explained how recess is an integral part of the Finnish education system. He described how the time students spend in unstructured play gives them a much needed mental break. Unstructured play also provides practice in "unstandardized skills" and dispositions like communication, conflict resolution, problem solving, collaboration, leadership, empathy, strategizing, and creativity (Tienken, 2017).

Lee (1915) summed it up best when he wrote, "it is the supreme seriousness of play that gives it its educational importance. Play . . . is the most serious thing in life. . . . Play builds the child. . . . Play is thus the essential part of education" (pp. 3–7). The importance of movement during the school day cannot be overstated. Dr. John Ratey (2013), clinical professor of psychiatry at Harvard Medical School, detailed three important outcomes of exercise on learning in his book *Spark*: (1) improved alertness, (2) increased ability to store new knowledge, and (3) aids the development of brain cells involved in long-term memory.

Recess of the Mind

Traditional outdoor recess is not the only type of recess that school leaders can foster. One 20-minute outdoor recess a day is hardly enough to provide students the mental breaks needed to function at high levels. Students are under more academic stress today then ever before. Students receive heavy doses of static academic content and are deprived of aesthetic subjects that allow the mind to open, think creatively, and refresh.

School leaders need to expand their idea of recess to include activities that provide children mental breaks throughout the day. This can be done through a few minutes of meditation, yoga, mindset training, and short movement activities in the classroom.

Options for Recess of the Mind

Regardless of how active the learning is in the classroom, all students can benefit from stepping away and clearing the mind. Outdoor recess is but one option. Many options exist for school leaders and educators to foster recess of the mind on small and large scales and to provide students the mental space they need to operate at high levels of concentration and task engagement.

Regardless of how active the learning is in the classroom, all students can benefit from stepping away and clearing the mind.

Meditation

Contemplative education, known as meditation in the school context, is broadly defined as purposefully regulating one's attention through focusing on one's thoughts, emotions, and body states (Black, Milam, & Sussman, 2009). General mindfulness and mindfulness-based stress reduction programs are some of the most common types of meditation found in schools, although there are many types of meditation ranging from transcendental meditation to Zen.

General mindfulness programs in schools commonly focus attention on positive feelings and dispositions such as calmness, tranquility, and awareness of being and do not have a religious connotation. Mindfulness stress reduction programs help students to focus their attention on the present to reduce distractions and worry. Strategies often include breathing exercises, body awareness exercises, and forms of relaxation yoga.

Breathing exercises are often used to teach students to use breathing as an attention anchor to help students draw their attention from worry and stress to something they can control and to eliminate distractions to clear the mind (Zylowska et al., 2008). The importance of an attention anchor consistently shows up in the research literature as a key component of meditation.

There exist various types of commercial products and also a wide range of free video and audio resources on the Internet for school leaders to learn more about meditation and work with their staff members to bring it into schools. Common benefits of mindfulness meditation programs include decreases in student stress and anxiety and increases in self-regulation behaviors and self-concept (Waters, Barsky, Ridd, & Allen, 2015).

Results from nine studies conducted since 2005 in the United States, Canada, England, and Australia revealed positive effects of general mindfulness programs and mindfulness-based stress reduction programs. The frequency and duration of the programs ranged from 43 minutes two times per week to 10-minute sessions twice per day (Waters et al., 2015).

Yoga

The existing research on the influence of yoga programs in schools suggests positive benefits to student well-being, similar to those derived from mindfulness programs, and students can also receive physical benefits, depending on the type of yoga practiced. The most common types of yoga programs used in schools are ones that include movement and poses and ones that focus on the mind and use breathing exercises and meditation or relaxation techniques (Serwacki & Cook-Cottone, 2012).

The Transformative Life Skills (TLS) program (Frank & Bose, 2014) is an example of an evidence-based curriculum being used in some schools to teach middle school and high school students strategies for personal well-being and stress management. The TLS is a concrete example of a comprehensive yoga program in which breathing, movement, postures, and meditation are integrated and explicitly taught through a formalized curriculum.

Move It!

Structured meditation and yoga programs might not be possible in all schools for various reasons, but school leaders can encourage and support the use of basic movement in classrooms. Students can benefit from simply getting a three-minute stretch break at the end of a lesson or by participating in one of the many Internet-based get-up-and-move videos, like those offered by GoNoodle®.

School leaders can also encourage and support the use of flexible seating materials that allow students to bounce, wiggle, and swing their feet. Various types of stools, floor rockers, scoop rockers, and other ergo-seating options that allow movement while sitting can all be used to eliminate the sedentary state of traditional education settings.

Beyond physical seating options, there exist things like bouncy bands that attach to traditional desks and chairs that allow students to bounce their feet on giant rubber band-like material as they are seated. Used often with students who have attention deficit hyperactivity disorder, the bands would benefit many students (and this author!) by allowing them to move throughout a lesson without disturbing others.

Recess of the Mind at Work

The crush of myopic education accountability policy prioritizes test preparation and test taking over the mental and physical health and well-being of children. School leaders are sometimes actively discouraged to provide students more recess or access to physical education; arts programs; and opportunities to reflect, decompress, and center themselves for fear of losing time on test preparation. But, examples abound of school leaders and teachers making time for recess of the mind.

S.W.A.G.

The Social Wellness for Academic Growth (SWAG) program operates in the Atlantis School in New Jersey, a grades PreK–2 school in which 70% of students come from military families from the local joint military base. The SWAG program works to help students manage and remove physical, social, and emotional barriers associated with military life that decrease wellness.

According to Principal Michelle Stecchini, all students and staff participate in a 45-minute guided SWAG session per month, and teachers have resources for daily 5- to 10-minute activities that are completed during morning meetings. SWAG activities encompass a mixture of yoga, meditation, and movement. Techniques such as breathing exercises, legs up the wall, kind wishes, and positive affirmations are all used. Each classroom has a "take a break" station for students to use as needed during the day. Teachers also purposefully schedule time after lunch and recess for students to regroup and center.

There has been a noticeable decrease in behavioral referrals as educators and students learn how to better understand themselves and others. Students report that they use the strategies in class and at home, which suggests an increase in internal locus of control.

Mindfulness in Nanuet

The Nanuet School District, in Rockland County, New York, implemented a K–12 program aimed at helping students develop mindfulness and overall personal well-being. District school leader Dr. Kevin McCahill described the program as one that helps students increase control over their outlooks and dispositions by focusing on the "here-and-now" through self-awareness and attention to nonjudgmental thinking based on inquiry and kindness.

The program is layered with a district vision that is operationalized within a schoolwide framework. Each school has monthly assemblies for each grade level that teach a variety of mindfulness exercises conducted by trained staff members who use singing bowls to facilitate the assemblies. The school psychologist implements a series of classroom-based lessons in science about the relationship between mindfulness and how the brain works.

Subject area classroom teachers incorporate "mindful moments" in the classroom via 1- to 2-minute exercises such as using singing bowls to facilitate meditation, focus attention, and to manage and dissipate stress. Students also use short movement sequences to refresh their bodies and minds. Teachers often implement the "mindful moments" as part of a morning routine and during transitions between classes, after lunch recess, and before certain types of lessons like those associated with the writing process and reading comprehension.

Yoga is practiced in the physical education classes, and every teacher in the schools received Yoga4Classrooms® materials. The school counselors use mindfulness during their group and individual counseling sessions. Teachers receive monthly outlines for mindfulness strategies, and each classroom is equipped with meditation bells. There is also an outdoor education center that includes a mindfulness gazebo where classes can go and practice. The Nanuet program has evolved to the point in which students are leading the mindfulness exercises with their peers in some classes.

Well-Being in White Plains

The White Plains School District, located about 30 miles north of New York City, serves a population of approximately 7,000 students. The district embarked on a program aimed at strengthening overall student and staff well-being, academically, socially, and emotionally through thoughtful integration of mindfulness techniques and opportunities throughout the K–12 education program.

Superintendent Dr. Joseph Ricca explained that educators and stakeholders in the district recognized that the traditional academic program was no longer meeting all the needs of students. The evolution of brain development science and human development science has consistently demonstrated that there is so much more to learning and overall growth and development than just academics, and the academic part of education can be inhibited when social and emotional needs are not met.

Students and staff of the White Plains School District participate in mindfulness activities such as yoga, meditation, aerobics, and group meetings where students talk about stressors and concerns, all in an attempt to try to shine a light on self-care and lifelong strategies students and staff can use to increase well-being. The staff and community view education as a journey not a destination, and a critical component of that journey is personal well-being and the well-being of others.

In addition to school-based resources, the school principals collaborate with the parent and teacher associations and community partners to bring additional community resources such as artists in residence and poets in residence to add aesthetic mindfulness and appreciation to the program. The superintendent explained that part of the program is about helping students to better understand themselves and others and being open to other ideas and perspectives.

Charting a Course in Pennsylvania

Principal Steven Lin of the Fort Zeller Elementary School began the process of making sports psychology mindfulness a component of the physical education program through techniques like self-centering breathing as a cool-down strategy. Focusing and breathing activities are ideally suited to help students be mindful about successful performance and to derive greater control over their bodies, and the idea melds well with the sports-minded region of Pennsylvania in which the school is located. Lin and his teachers are expanding the idea of mindful performance to the visual arts classes as well by teaching the "art" of being intentionally present, because like sports, the arts are performance-based subject areas that require focus and attention.

So What? Understanding the Big Picture of Recess of the Mind

This section provides leaders with an example critique for recess of the mind viewed through the reflective questions from the six lenses of the critique framework.

Figure 7.1 • Six Lenses of Critique

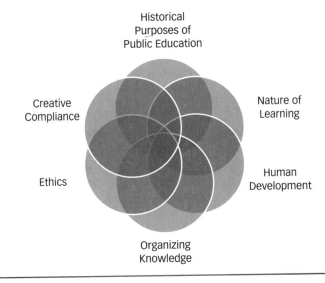

Historical
Purposes of
Public Education

Creative
Compliance

Nature of
Learning

Ethics

Human
Development

Organizing
Knowledge

1. How well does the/would the implementation of *recess of the mind* increase opportunities for students to take advantage of the unifying and specializing functions of public education?

The unifying function of public school brings together diverse peoples around democratic ideals and working toward the greater good of improving one's self, community, culture, and country. Recess of the mind can improve self-regulation, concentration, self-efficacy, self-image, brain development, attitude, the ability to focus and attend, and overall emotional, social, and physical well-being.

Being able to reflect on one's own being and have greater control over one's attitude, emotions, and actions allows students to better understand themselves and others. Understanding and empathy are key ingredients of working for the democratic greater good because they allow us to see the world through the eyes of others, and it is that vision of another's world that helps us to unify as a people.

Understanding and empathy are key ingredients of working for the democratic greater good because they allow us to see the world through the eyes of others, and it is that vision of another's world that helps us to unify as a people.

The specializing function of public school provides students with the focused subject area content and unstandardized skills and dispositions (Tienken, 2017) necessary to live economically, socially, and emotionally vibrant lives. Higher levels of well-being allow students to make the most of their education resources, where students who experience lower levels of well-being are unable to make full use of the resources provided (Scherrer, 2014). This is a major component of the "achievement gap," because the achievement gap is really an opportunity-to-learn gap (Carter & Welner, 2013).

Recess of the mind strategies increase overall levels of student well-being that then translate into students being able to design, customize, personalize, and make overall better use of their education experiences.

> 2. What are the implications of the reform for those inside and outside the range of the developmental stage upon which the reform rests?

Recess of the mind fits within what Yong Zhao (2018) termed *personalized education*. Personalized education focuses on "enhancing students' strengths and supporting their passions. It is rooted in the belief that all children have the potential and need to be great" (p. 67). Personalized education is different from personalized learning, which is focused on identifying weaknesses and "fixing" the student. Personalized education is about cultivating potential and passion, therefore it is naturally open-ended and accessible to all developmental stages. There are no prerequisites for potential!

Recess of the mind accommodates all developmental stages because it allows children to be themselves, come as they are, and participate in ways in which they are able and interested. Of course some students will get more benefits out of meditation, yoga, and movement by applying themselves more than others, but over time, all students benefit because the culture of the school begins to change to one that is more accepting and focused on cultivation of talent instead of measuring deficiencies.

> 3. How well does the reform acknowledge the target audience (e.g., student, teacher) as an active constructor of meaning who brings prior knowledge to the situation?

Recess of the mind strategies and techniques put students in the driver's seat in terms of taking control of their lives. They develop a sense of self that creates higher levels of intrinsic motivation. Students are better prepared to deal with difficult situations and capitalize upon positive ones. Students learn that they can control events around them and that they have the power to make meaningful connections to academic, social, and emotional opportunities. They can draw upon their past to make a better future.

4. How well does the reform allow the organization and delivery of knowledge to be customized to maximize active learning and participation of the target audience?

Recess of the mind strategies and techniques are naturally customized at the point of contact, the student, by the student. The student learns how to take total control of the experiences, whether they be physical, social, or emotional. Traditional recess, meditation, yoga, mindfulness, and simple movement in classrooms are all predicated on student control and personalizing education, as described by Zhao (2018).

Ethics

5. How does the reform impact the recognition and respect of stakeholders' dignity as human beings and the right to exhibit unique characteristics and behaviors?

Recess of the mind can be deeply personal. For example, the traditional playground recess is a deeply personal space. Students are interacting on personal levels, without the constant monitoring and funnelling of behavior from a teacher that is often seen in rigid classrooms. Kids are kids on the playground in all their uniqueness and love of life. They are their own person at that moment.

Yoga, mindfulness, meditation, and general movements in the classroom also provide students the safe emotional space to connect to themselves on a deeper level and initiate an ethic of self-care. They can privately manage and cope with stressors, develop physical and emotional independence, and become more reflective about ideas, feelings, and thoughts that they normally do not have time to attend to in a traditional school day spent shuffling from class to class and listening or being told what to think.

Creative Compliance

1. What creative compliance strategies can I take within my sphere of influence that will help to revise the education reform or capitalize upon it to become more aligned with the Curriculum Paradigm and the ethics of justice and care, in order to do less harm and more good?

Although the general well-being of children should not be controversial, a good deal of controversy can surround mindfulness, yoga, meditation, and any strategies associated with recess of the mind, what is collectively called social-emotional learning. Politics, ideology, misunderstanding, and skepticism can create a climate in which recess of the mind programs are branded as brainwashing, political propaganda, religion, or thought control. In such cases, creative compliance strategies can help to overcome the negative forces.

Piloting Followed by Negotiation

School leaders who face negativity and resistance to recess of the mind might first opt to pilot less intrusive activities, based on the school leader's understanding of the local context. A small-scale pilot can help create positive examples that demonstrate that the negative rumors and hearsay are not true.

The successful examples from the pilot can then be used to negotiate with district leaders to increase the size and scope of the program following a logical, multiyear timeline to allow people to become comfortable with the program. Small groups in physical education or a group of willing teachers in a school can form the basis of a pilot. For example, just one teacher on a middle school team can impact 100+ students at least once a day.

Circumventing

Messaging can be an important factor in communities that are suspicious of social-emotional learning. School leaders can use alternative terms such as academic focusing, sports psychology, or success visualization as euphemisms for mindfulness and meditation. Similarly, yoga can be conducted as part of "warm-up" exercises in physical education or the classroom. Classroom movement activities such as GoNoodle® generally do not carry negative connotations, so school leaders can simply start with those and keep them to the classroom level with willing teachers. School leaders are not required to announce a formal program or initiative, especially if it is small-scale use by small groups of teachers.

Try This!

- What are some examples in which recess of the mind is or can be used in your setting, and what can you do about it?

- What ethical dilemmas are created?

- Which creative compliance strategies can you use to increase the use of recess of the mind, and why would they be effective?

- What opportunities exist to capitalize on recess of the mind or redefine it so that it increases educational opportunities and quality for all students?

- What potential problems do you foresee, and what can you do about them now and for a Plan B?

Leadership Take-Away: Recess of the Mind

The size of the pilot or program does not necessarily matter. What matters is finding ways to create the programs that will increase student well-being; however, that can be accomplished in your specific context.

Next Steps

The unifying idea that helps define recess of the mind is student well-being. Many pathways exist for school leaders to initiate well-being programs. Students spend more time involved in on-task academic behaviors, at earlier ages, than ever before. Students are expected to be "on-task" for upward of 300 minutes a day. That level of intense focus can become counterproductive, and I believe it is developmentally inappropriate. School leaders must step up and provide the recess of the mind that students need to not only increase academic achievement but also to increase personal well-being.

Chapter 8

CASE STUDY 5

Problem- and Project-Based Learning

This case presents a general critique of the promising practice of problem- and project-based learning (PBL) and provides school leaders with ways PBL can be promoted and used effectively. John Dewey (1916) suggested that the best type of teaching is found in lessons that connect the nature of knowledge, academic/social/emotional content, to students' life experiences, passions, and interests through active learning experiences. He went on to say that the best method of instruction is when educators "give students something to do instead of something to learn" (p. 455). Dewey explained that curricula and instruction that treat each lesson as an independent experience, separate from other lessons and content, and unrelated to the interests or the personal experiences of the students represents the least effective types of learning in which students can engage.

Dewey (1916) stated that active learning respects the nature of the learner as an active constructor of meaning because it "puts the student in the habitual attitude of finding points of contact and mutual bearings" so students can connect the content and skills to their lived experiences and transfer that content and skills to other situations to solve problems in their lives (p. 117).

Importance of Active Learning

Students are part of an ecosystem that includes economic, political, cultural, racial, ethnic, environmental, religious, and general sociocivic diversity. Curriculum design, development, and implementation needs to go beyond the static knowledge and rudimentary skills needed during the industrial revolution. A static one-size-fits-all set of curricular expectations, also known as curriculum content standards, will not prepare students for an uncertain future.

There is no evidence that one set of curricular expectations or standards produce superior results that correlate to meaningful academic, economic, sociocivic, or avocational measures that are important in an innovation economy or democratic society. Unfortunately, most of the content embedded in today's state standards harkens back to the recommendations of the National Education Association's Committee of Ten (1893) and Committee of Fifteen (1895) and represents agrarian-era thinking.

Curricula designed, developed, and implemented for students living in a diverse global society must be less standardized and connected to the unique needs and contexts of the students compelled to experience it. But what should the content of such curricula include?

Historical Support for Active Learning

The authors of Volume II of the Eight Year Study (Giles, McCutchen, & Zechiel, 1942) suggested two broad functions that should be included in an educational program to help prepare students to be participative members in a democratic, global society:

> (1) the educational program should aid the learner in making effective adaptation to his environment in all its major aspects physical, economic, and social; (2) the educational program should develop in each individual those personal characteristics that will enable him to participate effectively in the preservation and extension of the culture. (p. 5)

Dewey (1910) proposed a specific type of thinking that should be part of a comprehensive educational program like the one described above: reflective thinking. Some refer to it as higher order thinking. He presented two components of reflective thinking that envelop higher order thinking: (1) a state of perplexity, hesitation, doubt (or problem); and (2) an act of search or investigation directed toward bringing to light further facts which serve to corroborate or to nullify the suggested belief [problem solving] (p. 3).

Dewey explained that a focus on knowledge acquisition instead of higher order thinking to solve authentic problems is caused by a mismatch between curriculum and instruction and understanding the natural development of children. He wrote, "In all cases, the adult environment is accepted as a standard for the child. . . . Natural instincts are either disregarded or treated as nuisances—as obnoxious traits to be suppressed, or at all events to be brought into conformity with external standards . . . conformity is made equivalent to uniformity" (p. 145).

The need exists to connect academic content to the child. The most effective method for that is PBL and instruction.

Defining PBL

A practical working definition of PBL comes from Mergendoller, Markham, Ravitz, and Larmer (2006, p. 583), as cited in *Rigorous PBL by Design* (McDowell, 2017, p. 2): "Series of complex tasks that include planning and design, problem solving, decision making, creating artifacts, and communicating results." Think of a PBL as a comprehensive activity, or series of activities, that allow students to actively inquire, create solutions, and take action on a problem or scenario that has relevance to their lives or interests.

For the purposes of this chapter, the term *PBL* is used for problem-based activities and projects. However, PBLs as suggested in the chapter should relate to socially conscious issues in some way to operationalize the connections between student experience, education, and democratic participation that is a historical function of schooling.

Designing PBLs

The good news is that PBL has been around a long time. Also known as the "problem method," as described in Volume II of the Eight Year Study, PBL has a straightforward framework. Giles et al. (1942, p. 15) identified seven parts:

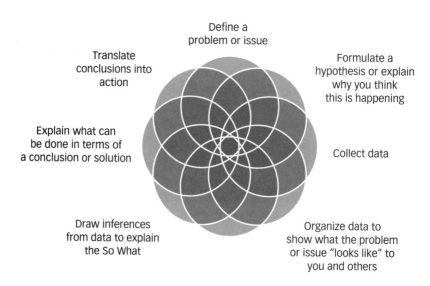

Define a problem or issue

Translate conclusions into action

Formulate a hypothesis or explain why you think this is happening

Explain what can be done in terms of a conclusion or solution

Collect data

Draw inferences from data to explain the So What

Organize data to show what the problem or issue "looks like" to you and others

Dewey recommended an eighth component: reflection. Student reflection on the problems associated with the suggested actions or solutions to the problems is crucial. Achilles, Reynolds, and Achilles (1997) termed reflection in the context of problem solving as the *problem of the solution*, or considering the consequences of solutions.

Learning does not get more active or authentic than a socially conscious PBL based on student interests and passions. Student interest in the topic makes it easier to integrate all that static knowledge contained in state content standards. The PBL is like the bridge that connects the static world of content to the active world of the child, and that bridge makes learning more fun, engaging, and student centered.

Creating Topics for PBLs

The educational context of the student is the garden of socially conscious PBLs. Dewey (1916) recommended that selection of a problem for study must be "an outgrowth of existing conditions. It must be based upon a consideration of what is already going on; upon the resources and difficulties of the situation" (p. 298). Dewey's advice helps educators to ensure that some level of student interest, passion, and need are incorporated into the curricula and instruction. Students are naturally drawn to inquiry about socially conscious problems.

Whether it is an issue of fairness and equity, greed, personal relationships, personal rights, communities, climate, government, the environment, conflict, or justice, students are inclined to engage socially and emotionally in such topics. The selection of a problem or issue based on careful consideration of what is already occurring in society addresses a pressing social force and aligns with another important aspect of the Curriculum Paradigm: the nature of the learner as an active constructor of meaning. Collecting facts and isolated skills for the sake of knowledge acquisition or regurgitation on a standardized test does not satisfy students' natural curiosity and drive to experience life, learn, and to actively apply their learning to influence life situations.

The Power of PBL

The use of developmentally appropriate, socially conscious problems as a foundation for curriculum and instruction is an evidence-informed and concrete way for educators to begin to organize knowledge for study. Problems are also an effective means for students to encounter unstandardized skills and dispositions and ultimately to learn and transfer those skills and dispositions to authentic contexts in intelligent and responsible ways in order to grow as individuals and contribute to the greater good (Tienken, 2017). Some unstandardized skills and dispositions fostered by PBL include those listed in Figure 8.1.

Students' thinking about the problems associated with proposed solutions adds a purposeful reflective aspect to the PBLs and might

Figure 8.1 • Unstandardized Skills and Dispositions

Active listening	Big picture thinking	Cognitive nimbleness	Collaboration	Communicating
Compassion	Compromise	Confidence	Conscientiousness	Consensus Building
Courage	Creativity	Critical consideration of information	Critique	Cultural literacy
Curiousness	Design thinking	Dignity	Empathy	Entrepreneurial thinking
Environmental stewardship	Ethics	Fairness	Friendship	Goal setting
Happiness	Humility	Imagination	Innovation	Integrity
Kindness	Leadership	Love	Motivation	Network building
Openness	Persistence	Potential problem analysis	Pride	Problem finding
Problem solving	Reflection	Resilience	Self-control	Self-efficacy
Sharing	Social consciousness	Strategizing	Taking action	Timeliness
Togetherness	Understanding others	Verbal acuity	Visioning	Worldliness

Figure 8.1 adapted from Tienken (2017). *Defying standardization: Creating curriculum for an uncertain future.* Lanham, MD: Rowman and Littlefield.

represent the most impactful aspect of the method. Reflection provides openings for students to consider the potential consequences of their actions and facilitates the creation of a feedback loop because reflection can generate additional student questions, and the problems associated with the solutions become new problems for future study or enrichment.

Students' thinking about the problems associated with proposed solutions adds a purposeful reflective aspect to the PBLs and might represent the most impactful aspect of the method.

Dewey (1916) commented that "every end becomes a means of carrying activity further as soon as it is achieved" (p. 303). The learning never ends. The problems under study can become increasingly layered and extend across grade levels and subject areas. Problems can act as a unifying core from which to organize a school's entire curriculum on a larger scale.

PBL as Powerful Inquiry

Multiple structures exist for inquiry-based learning via PBL on a continuum ranging from teacher-centered to student-centered. School leaders can use PBL work with staff to match the PBL structure to educators' level of comfort with inquiry-based approaches.

Confirmation Inquiry is a teacher-centered approach in which students confirm a principle through an activity in which the results are known in advance (Bianchi & Bell, 2008). This type of inquiry is most often seen in science classes but can be used as an introductory structure for initial PBL experiences.

Structured inquiry is a semi-teacher-centered approach that provides some level of student voice and choice (Salim & Tiawa, 2015). The teacher provides the question or problem and the procedures for a structured inquiry PBL, but the students create a solution or explanation supported by evidence gathered during the study of the topic. Guided inquiry moves the inquiry process further toward a student-centered approach. Students investigate a teacher-presented question or problem, but they use student-designed or student-selected procedures (Kuhlthau, Maniotes, & Caspari, 2015).

Open Inquiry represents a student-centered approach in which students investigate student-formulated questions or problems and use student-designed or selected procedures (Bianchi & Bell, 2008). Open Inquiry allows students to identify problems they find based on observations or interests. The continuum of inquiry allows educators to choose a structure that best accommodates their context, student interests, and resources.

Rigorous PBL by Design (McDowell, 2017) provides excellent resources for designing and planning PBLs to accommodate every type of inquiry. McDowell also provides graphic organizers and charts that educators can use for start to finish planning of their PBL experiences.

Finding PBLs

Ready-made PBLs and ideas for PBLs abound. Sites like PBLU.org, the Buck Institute for Education *Out of the Gate* (http://www.bie.org/ootg), and the Intel© Teaching Ideas Showcase are just some examples of places to find PBL's. I also curate my own Scoopit© page with over 50 other websites with PBLs: https://www.scoop.it/t/problem-based-learning-by-christopher-tienken?page=1.

Don't reinvent the wheel. Find one that works for your school. Teachers can easily customize the ready-made PBLs to fit their students' unique needs and interests. Educators do not have to start from scratch. Schools like High Tech High and High Tech Middle in California have dozens of teacher-created PBLs loaded onto their school websites for free download as well. Find ways to give teachers the gift of time.

Making It Happen

Start small! One small project per marking period is a great start! Use the power of the faculty to get PBLs happening across a school. For example, a middle school content team can create a small-scale PBL for each marking period and ensure that all students experience at least four PBL opportunities a year! School leaders can supply time during faculty meetings, professional development days, or team meetings and help design projects with the teachers. Then, get PBLs inserted into the curriculum so everyone has access and resource support.

Each PBL should culminate with students taking action in some way and then reflecting on the potential consequences of that action. Taking action can be something as simple as raising awareness about an issue with a 45-second video Public Service Announcement (PSA). PBLs do not need to be long-term events to effectively engage students in active learning. School leaders can carve out time for PBL planning and support it with coaching and collaboration.

So What? Understanding the Big Picture of PBL

This section provides leaders with an example critique of PBL viewed through the reflective questions from the six lenses of the critique framework.

Figure 8.2 • Six Lenses of Critique

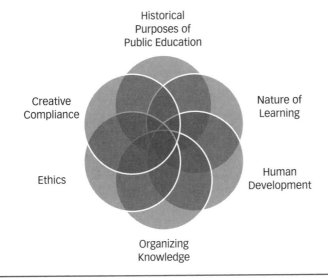

Historical Purposes of Public Education

Creative Compliance

Nature of Learning

Ethics

Human Development

Organizing Knowledge

1. How well does the/would the reform address the three historical aims of education?

PBL is an instructional homerun in terms of fostering academic, sociocivic, and avocational knowledge, skills, and dispositions.

Almost any academic content can be integrated into a well-chosen problem, project, or scenario, and the real-world context allows for multiple unstandardized skills and dispositions to be developed. PBL can operationalize Dewey's (1929) vision of the sociocivic role of public education in nurturing a democracy:

For the creation of a democratic society we need an educational system where the process of moral intellectual development is in practice as well as in theory a cooperative transaction of inquiry engaged in by free, independent human beings who treat ideas and the heritage of the past as means and methods for the further enrichment of life, quantitatively and qualitatively, who use the good attained for the discovery and establishment of something better. (p. 84)

Almost any academic content can be integrated into a well-chosen problem, project, or scenario, and the real-world context allows for multiple unstandardized skills and dispositions to be developed.

The use of socially conscious problems and projects moves students from observers of democracy to active participants, based on the purposeful application of academic knowledge and skills: transfer of learning. For those who value a participative democracy in which people from all races, ethnicities, religions, sexual orientation, and social classes critique ideas, think creatively, and are able to lead, the historic purposes of public education are not to be dismissed as old fashioned or rejected as no longer relevant.

Dewey (1916) wrote that all citizens should participate actively in the democratic governing of the nation, and the public school is the place where diverse peoples can become introduced to the American democratic traditions. The public school is, in essence, the only social institution in the United States in which the vast majority of youth pass through for an extended number of years. Thus, it is the only social institution in which the entire future generation of citizens can learn how to actively participate in the governing of their democratic country, and PBL is a method to create collaboration and communication around issues of democracy.

2. In what ways does the proposal account for the various stages of human development of the target audience, and where is it lacking?

PBL, when created and implemented in ways that allow for multiple solutions or conclusions, is naturally differentiated by readiness. This means that 20 students can give 20 different responses, at the level of sophistication in which they are ready, and all be engaged in personal development of their academic, sociocivic, and avocational skills and dispositions.

PBL fosters open-ended thinking. Open-ended thinking allows all students to approach learning in ways that work for them. When PBL is created with options for multiple types of student output (taking action), it accommodates a variety of student learning needs, passions, and interests. In short, PBL can be designed to be developmentally pliable to accommodate all different degrees of academic, sociocivic, and avocational readiness.

3. How well does the reform acknowledge the target audience (e.g., student, teacher) as an active constructor of meaning who brings prior knowledge to the situation?

PBL implemented in structured inquiry, guided inquiry, and open inquiry structures allows for student voice and action at some point in the PBL. All PBL, when implemented according to the problem-method framework, places students in the position of active constructor of meaning. Students inquire, take action, and reflect on their potential consequences of their actions.

4. How well does the reform provide for the connection of the mandated content or process to the existing knowledge and skill set of the target audience?

PBL is a natural way to bring life to static content and connect that content to student interest, prior knowledge, and experiences. PBL provides the vehicle to infuse formal academic content into the sphere of student experience.

Ethics

5. How do the intended or unintended impacts of the reform impact individuals, groups, or the educational community as it pertains to equity, social justice, or recognition as a human being?

Socially conscious PBL aligns with Dewey's view of the ethics of justice because it helps the individual come to understand how his or her own behavior influences the common good. PBLs are the perfect vehicle to engage students in the study of topics like equity, social justice, and human rights. Engaging students in socially conscious PBLs can help build empathy and compassion, which in turn can lead to greater understanding and concern for equity and social justice.

Creative Compliance

1. What creative compliance strategies can I take within my sphere of influence that will help to revise the education reform to become more aligned with the Curriculum Paradigm and the ethics of justice and care, in order to do less harm and more good, or to capitalize on positive aspects of the reform?

It might hard to believe, but in some places, PBL is restricted by the use of prescriptive curriculum products or the misplaced belief that PBL is not compatible with state-mandated curriculum standards. How can school leaders capitalize on the strengths of PBL when they work in environments that are hostile to PBL?

Circumventing

Circumventing is the preferred response in situations that include prescriptive curriculum or an organizational ideology that excludes PBL, just like with recess of the mind, messaging, or rebranding, can be an effective first tool for leaders in environments that exclude PBL. School leaders do not have to use the term *PBL*. They can simply call it *activity design* but use the characteristics and parameters of PBL as the design template. Activities are a part of almost every lesson, and teachers can work on *activity design* at any time. School leaders are not required to announce a formal program or initiative because activity design is not new.

Circumventing prescriptive programs can be trickier because the stakes for the teachers and school leader can be higher in terms of disciplinary action and classroom evaluation ratings from administrators who come from outside the school (district supervisors, superintendent, etc.). However, short PBLs can be designed to complement prescriptive programs so that all students can still reap some benefits.

Teachers can implement the activities during the normal course of the lesson on most occasions. They would not be able to circumvent announced classroom evaluations of the implementation of the prescriptive program, and it could be difficult to circumvent unannounced evaluations or walk-through visitations. I have known teachers who would have the prescriptive program out and on the students' desks while doing PBLs and would switch to that program if an external administrator appeared. School leaders need to give teachers permission to circumvent in this way and take responsibility should questions arise.

Negotiation

Negotiation would be considered a high-risk option in this situation because the school leader must state his or her intentions to deviate in some way from the prescription. If the negotiation fails, the school leader's supervisor will know the leader's intentions and most likely begin monitoring. Deciding whether to negotiate comes down to the school leader's personal relationship with the decision maker and knowledge of how the decision maker might respond to the negotiation.

The point to be negotiated is the inclusion of some activity-based lessons within the scripted program. The messaging needs to be clear but not too specific in terms of frequency or duration. The goal is to get the decision maker to approve the idea of activities, not the specific parameters.

Try This!

- What are some examples in which PBL is or can be used in your setting, and what can you do about it?

- What ethical dilemmas are created?

- Which creative compliance strategies can you use to increase the use of PBL, and why would they be effective?

- What opportunities exist to capitalize on PBL or redefine it so that it increases educational opportunities and quality for all students?

- What potential problems do you foresee, and what can you do about them now and for a Plan B?

Leadership Take-Away: PBL

Doing something consistently, regardless of how extensive, is better than consistently doing nothing. Collaborate with staff to do PBL on some scale.

Doing something consistently, regardless of how extensive, is better than consistently doing nothing. Collaborate with staff to do PBL on some scale.

Next Steps

Dewey said it best in terms of how powerful active learning can be:

> Careful inspection of methods which are permanently successful in formal education . . . will reveal that they depend for their efficiency upon the fact that they go back to the type of the situation which causes reflection out of school in ordinary life. They give the pupils something to do, not something to learn; and the doing is of such a nature as to demand thinking, or the intentional noting of connections; learning naturally results. (pp. 442–443)

If you connect content to students in meaningful ways, you will get meaningful results, and learning will occur naturally.

Chapter 9

FINAL ISSUES

Issues: There is no shortage of challenging education reform issues confronted by public school leaders. The list seems to grow each year. Accountability schemes, educator evaluation programs, standardization of curriculum and assessment, contradictory policymaker expectations, and influences from international testing programs are just some topics that exert political pressure via rhetoric and education reform policy proposals. School leaders must regularly navigate multiple policy issues to remain focused on the daily commitment to providing a quality education to all students.

The array of issues that rain down upon educators can seem overwhelming without a framework from which to make sense of them. The information communicated via the mainstream media and some of the most commonly read education publications sometimes provides unclear, contradictory, or simply factually incorrect information and rhetoric regarding education reform policies and programs.

Spencer Returns

In 1883, Herbert Spencer posed the age-old question to educators: What knowledge is of most worth? Many people still debate the question today in terms of curriculum and testing. But what about education reforms? What education reform is of most worth? Educators have traditionally struggled with answering that question due to a lack of a usable tool to critique reforms.

The framework provided in this book provides leaders a tool with which they can conduct systematic, evidence-informed critiques of reforms and take creative and ethical actions to capitalize on the positive aspects and limit the negative characteristics at the point of contact: the student.

Although the framework presented might not be able to determine which reform is of "most worth," it certainly can provide educators with a way to determine the educational and ethical efficacy of reforms so they can determine which reform or parts of a reform are of *most worth* to their schools.

It is difficult to predict the next "big" reform, but there is no doubt that education reform proposals will continue to arrive at the schoolhouse door unabated. The names and acronyms might change, but the underlying reform topics will be similar. The critique framework can be applied to any reform.

Top 10

Figure 9.1 presents the Top 10 reform topics that will continue to influence education policy and practice in the future and the lenses of the critique framework that school leaders can use to evaluate them. Some reforms are so big or ambiguous that it can be hard for leaders to know where to start their critique. The figure suggests the primary lenses that school leaders can use to critique a reform and the secondary lenses that can provide additional information.

For example, the historical purposes of education and the ethics of care and justice are the primary lenses a school leader can use to efficiently and effectively conduct an initial critique of *private school choice* reforms. Democracy and the greater good have always been at the forefront of the public education system. The Jeffersonian view of the role and responsibility of education was one of equity, progress, change, and evolution. Jefferson's well-known flaws in his thinking on racial equality notwithstanding, he did propose a public education system that would level the playing field between those that came from privileged backgrounds and those who did not have such advantages, so as to help society progress (Tienken & Orlich, 2013).

Private school choice violates the sociocivic, democratic functions of schooling because private school choice is based on the concept of consumerism, not democracy, and it fosters segregation and balkanization of groups.

The ethic of justice requires school leaders to consider the importance of the relationship between public school and a democratic society before determining their support for a reform that silos segments of the population most often by race and class. Public school is the only publicly funded and universally accessible social institution that provides a mechanism to socialize all future adults to democracy in diverse settings.

Figure 9.1 • Lenses for Critiquing the Top 10 Reforms

	Nature of the Learner	Nature of Knowledge	Human Development	Social Forces	Historical Purposes of Education	Ethic of Care	Ethic of Justice
1. Zero tolerance behavior policies	P	S	P	S	S	P	P
2. Standardized curricula content	P	P	P	S	S	S	P
3. Standardized testing-based accountability systems	S	P	P	S	P	P	P
4. Teacher evaluation based on standardized test scores	P	S	S	S	S	P	P
5. School leader evaluation based on standardized test scores	P	S	S	S	S	P	P
6. Problem- & project-based learning	P	P	P	P	P	S	S
7. Social emotional learning	P	S	P	S	P	P	P
8. Private school choice	S	S	S	S	P	S	P
9. Virtual K-12 schools	P	P	S	S	P	S	P
10. Special education inclusion & mainstreaming	S	S	P	S	P	P	P

P = Primary lens for critique

S = Secondary lens for critique

Crack the Code and Act!

School leaders do not have to embrace the defeatist attitude of "like it or not" when it comes to implementing education reforms. Understanding an issue is a good first step toward taking action on it. I hope that readers will find some support in the various chapters of this book so they can crack the code of education reform and change the trajectory of ineffective reforms and capitalize on the positive aspects of evidence-based reforms.

References

Dedication

Delonge, T. (2010). *Shove*. Love Part I. Rocket Science.

Introduction

Cremin, L. A. (1961). *The transformation of the school: Progressivism in American education*. New York, NY: Alfred A. Knopf.

Dewey, J. (1916/2009). *Democracy and education: An introduction to the philosophy of education*. Cedar Lake, MI: Readaclassic.

Tanner, D., & Tanner, L. N. (2007). *Curriculum development: Theory into practice*, 4th ed. New York, NY: Pearson.

Chapter 1

Buskey, F. C., & Pitts, E. M. (2013). The role of personal ethical checking in courageous school leadership. *NCPEA Education Leadership Review, 1*(3), 73-80.

Giles, H. H., McCutchen, S. P., & Zechiel, A. N. (1942). *Adventures in American education volume II: Exploring the curriculum*. New York, NY: Harper and Brothers.

Gross, S., & Shapiro, J. (2004). Using multiple ethical paradigms and turbulence theory in response to administrative dilemmas. *International Studies in Educational Administration 32*(2), 47–62.

Noddings, N. (1999). Care, justice, and equity. In M. Katz, N. Noddings, & K. Strike (Eds.), *Justice and caring: The search for common ground in education* (pp. 7-20). New York, NY: Teachers College Press.

RAND Corporation. (n.d.). *Education reform*. Retrieved April 24, 2019, from https://www.rand.org/topics/education-reform.html.

Rawls, J. (1971). *A theory of justice*. Cambridge, MA: Harvard University Press.

Starratt, R. J. (1991). Building an ethical school: A theory for practice in educational leadership. *Educational Administration Quarterly, 27*(2), 185-202.

Starratt, R. J. (2004). *Ethical leadership*. San Francisco, CA: Jossey-Bass.

Stefkovich, J., & Begley, P. T. (2007). Ethical school leadership: Defining the best interests of students. *Educational Management Administration & Leadership, 35*(2), 205-224. doi:10.1177/1741143207075389

Sullivan, W. M. (1986). *Reconstructing public philosophy*. Berkeley, CA: University of California Press.

Tienken, C. H., & Orlich, D. C. (2013). *The school reform landscape: Fraud, myth, and lies*. New York, NY: Rowman & Littlefield.

Zhao, Y. (2018). *Reach for greatness: Personalizable education for all children*. Thousand Oaks, CA: Corwin.

Chapter 2

Buskey, F. C., & Pitts, E. M. (2009). Training subversives: The ethics of leadership preparation. *Phi Delta Kappan, 91*(3), 57-61.

Buskey, F. C., & Pitts, E. M. (2013). Personal ethical checking in courageous school leadership. *NCPEA Education Leadership Review, 14*(3), 73-81.

Every Student Succeeds Act (ESSA), Pub. L. No. 114-95 § 114 Stat. 1177 (December 10, 2015).

Fountas, I., & Pinnell, G. S. (2016). *The Fountas and Pinnell literacy continuum, expanded edition: A tool for assessment, planning and teaching, PreK–8.* Portsmouth, NH: Heinenmann.

Grant, A. (2013, Nov. 6). 7 sneaky influence tactics you never saw coming. *Psychology Today.* Retrieved from https://www.psychologytoday.com/us/blog/give-and-take/201311/7-sneaky-influence-tactics-you-never-saw-coming.

He, M.F. (2016). Thriving in-between landscapes of education. *The Sophist's Bane, 8*(1), 47-56.

Hoy, W. K., & Tartar, J. C. (2007). *Leaders solving the problems of practice: Decision-making concepts, cases, and consequences,* 3rd ed. New York, NY: Pearson.

Jones, E. E. (1964). *Ingratiation: A social psychological analysis.* New York, NY: Appleton-Century-Crofts.

Kepner-Tregoe, Inc. (2013). Potential problem analysis. Retrieved from https://www.kepner-tregoe.com/linkservid/C8339742-D8F6-9A77-4011 D16AA6D2D37A/showMeta/0.

Stern, I., & Westphal, J. D. (2010). Stealthy footsteps to the boardroom: Executives' backgrounds, sophisticated influence behavior, and board appointments. *Administrative Sciences Quarterly, 55*(2), 278-319.

Chapter 3

Achilles, C. M., Reynolds, J. S., & Achilles, S. H. (1997). *Problem analysis: Responding to school complexity.* Larchmont, NY: Eye on Education.

Aikin, W. M. (1942). *The story of the eight-year study.* New York, NY: Harper.

Commission on the Reorganization of Secondary Education. (1918). *Cardinal principles of secondary education.* Washington, DC: U.S. Bureau of Education, Bulletin No. 35.

Dewey, J. (1897). My pedagogic creed. *School Journal, 54,* 77-80.

Dewey, J. (1899). *The school and society.* Chicago, IL: University of Chicago Press.

Dewey, J. (1902). *The child and the curriculum.* Chicago, IL: University of Chicago Press.

Dewey, J. (1910/1933). *How we think.* Lexington, MA: D.C. Heath.

Dewey, J. (1916). *Democracy and education.* New York, NY: Macmillan.

Dewey, J. (1959). Introduction to the uses of resources in education. In M. S. Dworkin (Ed.), *Dewey on education* (p. 31). New York, NY: Teachers College Press.

Dewey, J., & Tufts, J. H. (1908). *Ethics*. Chicago, IL: H. Holt & Co.

Gijbels, D., Dochy, F., Van den Bossche, P., & Segers, M. (2005). Effects of problem-based learning: A meta-analysis from the angle of assessment. *Review of Educational Research, 75*(1), 27-61.

Giles, H. H., McCutchen, S. P., & Zechiel, A. N. (1942). *Adventures in American education volume II: Exploring the curriculum*. New York, NY: Harper and Brothers.

Jersild, A. T., Thorndike, R. L., & Goldman, B. (1941). A further comparison of pupils in "activity" and "non-activity" schools. *Journal of Experimental Education, 9*, 307-309.

Kontra, C., Lyons, D. J., Fischer, S. M., & Bellock, S. L. (2015). Physical experience enhances science learning. *Psychological Science, 26*(6), 737-749.

Maslow, A. H. (1943). A theory of human motivation. *Psychological Review, 50*(4), 370–396.

Prince, M. (2004). Does active learning really work? A review of the research. *Journal of Engineering Education, 93*(3), 223-231.

Roemer, J. (1998). *Equality of opportunity*. Cambridge, MA: Harvard University Press.

Taba, H. (1962). *Curriculum development: Theory into practice*. New York, NY: Harcourt, Brace, & World, Inc.

Tanner, D. (2016). Jean Piaget's debt to John Dewey. *AASA Journal of Scholarship and Practice, 13*(1), 6-24.

Tanner, D., & Tanner, L. N. (2007). *Curriculum development: Theory into practice*, 4th ed. New York, NY: Pearson.

Thorndike, E. L. (1924). Mental discipline in high school studies. *Journal of Educational Psychology, 15*, 1-22, 98.

Tienken, C. H. (2017). *Defying standardization: Creating curriculum for an uncertain future*. Lanham, MD: Rowman and Littlefield.

Tyler, R. W. (1949). *Basic principles of curriculum and instruction*. Chicago, IL: University of Chicago Press.

Wang, M. C., Haertel, G. D., & Walberg, H. J. (1993). Toward a knowledge base for school learning. *Review of Educational Research, 63*(3), 249-294.

Ward, L. F. (1883). *Dynamic sociology* (Vol. 1). New York, NY: D. Appleton & Co.

Woolfolk, A., & Perry, N. E. (2011). *Child and adolescent development*. Upper Saddle River, NJ: Pearson.

Zhao, Y. (2018). *Reach for greatness: Personalizable education for all children*. Thousand Oaks, CA: Corwin.

Chapter 4

Aikin, W. M. (1942). *The story of the eight-year study with conclusions and recommendations*. New York, NY: Harper & Brothers.

Albert, R. S., & Runco, M. A. (1999). A history of research on creativity. In R. J. Sternberg (Ed.), *Handbook of creativity* (pp. 16-34). Cambridge, UK: Cambridge University Press.

Asia Society, Center for Global Education. (2015a). *Graduation performance system. Global leadership performance outcomes. Grade 5.* Retrieved from http://asiasociety.org/files/uploads/522files/globalleadership_5_outcomes .pdf.

Asia Society, Center for Global Education. (2015b). *Graduation performance system. Global leadership performance outcomes. Grade 10.* Retrieved from http://asiasociety.org/files/uploads/522files/globalleadership_10_out comes.pdf.

Bloom, B. S., Engelhart, M. D., Furst, E. J., Hill, W. H., & Krathwohl, D. R. (1956). *Taxonomy of educational objectives: Handbook I: Cognitive domain.* New York, NY: David McKay.

Booher-Jennings, J. (2005). Below the bubble: "Education triage" and the Texas accountability system. *American Education Research Journal, 42*(2), 231-268.

Carmichael, S. B., Martino, G., Porter-Magee, K., & Wilson, W. S. (2010). *The state of state standards and the common core.* Washington, DC: The Fordham Institute.

Dewey, J. (1899). *The school and society.* Chicago, IL: University of Chicago Press.

Dewey, J. (1916/2009). *Democracy and education: An introduction to the philosophy of education.* Cedar Lake, MI: Readaclassic.

Elementary Secondary Education Act, P.L. 89-10 § 79, Stat. 27 (April 11, 1965).

Every Student Succeeds Act, P.L. No. 114-95 § 114, Stat. 1177 (December 10, 2015). https://www.congress.gov/bill/114th-congress/senate-bill/1177/text.

Goals 2000 Educate America Act, Pub. L. No. 103-227, § 108, Stat. 125 (March 31, 1994). Retrieved from http://www2.ed.gov/legislation/GOALS2000/ TheAct/index.html.

Hechinger Report. (2010, March 25). *What is rigor?* Retrieved from http:// hechingerreport.org/content/experts-what-is-rigor_2109.

Hess, K., Carlock, D., Jones, B., & Walkup, J. (2009). *What exactly do "fewer, clearer, and higher standards" really look like in the classroom? Using a cognitive rigor matrix to analyze curriculum, plan lessons, and implement assessments.* Presentation at CCSSO, Detroit, MI, June 2009. Retrieved from http://www.nciea.org/publication_PDFs/cognitiverigorpaper_KH12.pdf.

Improving America's School Act of 1994, Pub. L. No. 103-382, § 108, Stat. 3518 (October 20, 1994). Retrieved from https://www.congress.gov/ bill/103rd-congress/house-bill/6/text.

Jersild, A. T., Thorndike, R. L., & Goldman, B. (1941). A further comparison of pupils in "activity" and "non-activity" schools. *Journal of Experimental Education, 9,* 307-309.

Lewis, A., & Smith, D. C. (1993). Defining higher order thinking. *Theory Into Practice: Teaching for Higher Order Thinking, 32*(3), 131-137.

National Governors Association Center for Best Practices, Council of Chief State School Officers. (2017). *Common Core State Standards: What parents should know.* Washington, DC: Author.

No Child Left Behind (NCLB), Act of 2001, Pub. L. No. 107-110, § 115, Stat. 1425 (January 8, 2002).

Padget, S. (2013). *Creativity and critical thinking*. Milton Park, UK: Routledge.

Partnership for Assessment of Readiness for College and Careers. (2014). *PARCC fact sheet*. Washington, DC: Author. Retrieved from www.parcconline.org/sites/parcc/files/PARCCFactSheetandFAQsBackgrounder_FINAL.pdf.

Pogrow, S. (1998). What is an exemplary program and why should anyone care? *Educational Researcher*, 22-29.

Pogrow, S. (2004). The missing element in reducing the gap: Eliminating the "blank stare". *Teachers College Record*. Retrieved from https://tcrecord.org/library/abstract.asp?contentid=11381.

Porter, A., McMaken, J., Hwang, J., & Yang, R. (2011). Common Core Standards: The new U.S. intended curriculum. *Educational Researcher, 40*(3), 103-116. doi:10.3102/0013189X11405038

Runco, M. A., & Chand, I. (1995). Cognition and creativity. *Educational Psychology Review, 7*(3), 243-267.

Runco, M. A., & Jaeger, G. J. (2012). The standard definition of creativity. *Creativity Research Journal, 1*, 92-96.

Sforza, D., Tienken, C. H., & Kim, E. (2016). A comparison of higher-order thinking between the Common Core State Standards and the 2009 New Jersey Content Standards in high school. *AASA Journal of Scholarship and Practice, 12*(4), 4-30.

Sternberg, R. (1999). *Handbook of creativity*. Cambridge, UK: Cambridge University Press.

Tanner, D., & Tanner, L. (2007). *Curriculum development: Theory into practice*. Upper Saddle River, NJ: Pearson.

Ward T. B., Smith, S. M., & Finke, R. A. (1999). Creative cognition. In R. J. Sternberg (Ed.), *Handbook of Creativity* (pp. 189-212). New York, NY: Cambridge University Press.

Webb, N. L. (1997). *Criteria for alignment of expectations and assessments in mathematics and science education* (Research Monograph No. 6). Washington, DC: Council of Chief State School Officers.

Webb, N. L., Alt, M., Ely, R., & Vesperman, B. (2005). *Web alignment tool training manual*. Wisconsin Center for Education Research. Retrieved from http://wat.wceruw.org/index.aspx.

Willis, M. (1961). *The guinea pigs after twenty years: A follow-up study of the class of 1938 of the University School of Ohio State*. Columbus, OH: Ohio State University Press.

Chapter 5

American Educational Research Association, American Psychological Association, & National Council on Measurement in Education. (2014). *Standards for educational and psychological testing* (7th ed.). Washington, DC: AERA.

Au, W. (2011). Teaching under the new Taylorism: High-stakes testing and the standardization of the 21st century curriculum. *Journal of Curriculum Studies, 43*(1), 25-45. doi:10.1080/00220272.2010.521261

Becker, G. S. (1993). *Human capital: A theoretical and empirical analysis, with special reference to education*, 3rd ed. Chicago: University of Chicago Press.

Berliner, D. (2011). Rational responses to high stakes testing: The case of curriculum narrowing and the harm that follows. *Cambridge Journal of Education, 41*(3), 287-302.

Bourdieu, P. (1986). The forms of capital. In J. G. Richardson (Ed.), *Handbook of theory and research for the sociology of education* (pp. 241-258). New York, NY: Greenwood Press.

Brandwein, D. (2011a). Army Alpha Intelligence Test. In J. A. Naglieri & S. Goldstein (Eds.), *Encyclopedia of child behavior and development* (pp. 141-142). New York, NY: Springer.

Brandwein, D. (2011b). Army Beta Intelligence Test. In J. A. Naglieri & S. Goldstein (Eds.), *Encyclopedia of child behavior and development* (pp. 142-143). New York, NY: Springer.

Bronfenbrenner, U. (1979). *The ecology of human development: Experiments by nature and design*. Cambridge, MA: Harvard University Press.

Caldwell, D. G. (2017). *The influence of socioeconomic, parental and district factors on the 2013 MCAS Grade 4 language arts and mathematics scores*. Seton Hall University Dissertations and Theses (ETDs). Paper 2251.

Coleman, J. T. (1988). Social capital in the creation of human capital. *The American Journal of Sociology, 94*, S95-S120.

Darnell, B. (2015). *The value of Iowa school district demographic data in explaining school district ITBS/ITED 3rd and 11th grade language arts and mathematics scores*. Seton Hall University Dissertations and Theses (ETDs). Paper 2075.

Dewey, J. (1929). *The sources of science of education*. New York, NY: Liveright.

Doherty, K. M., & Jacobs, S. (2015). *State of the States 2015: Evaluating teaching, leading and learning*. Washington, DC: National Council on Teacher Quality. Retrieved from http://www.nctq.org/dmsStage/StateofStates2015.

Flabbi, L., & Gatti, R. V. (2018). *A primer on human capital* (English). Policy Research working paper; no. WPS 8309. Washington, DC: World Bank Group.

Holcombe, R., Jennings, J., & Koretz, D. (2013). The roots of score inflation: An examination of opportunities in two states' tests. In G. Sunderman (Ed.), *Charting reform, achieving equity in a diverse nation* (pp. 163-189). Greenwich, CT: Information Age.

Joint Committee on Standards for Educational Evaluations. (1994). *The program evaluation standards: How to assess evaluations of educational programs*. Newbury Park, CA: Sage.

Jones, B. D. (2008). The unintended outcomes of high stakes testing. *Journal of Applied School Psychology, 23*(2), 65-86.

Koretz, D. (2009). *Measuring up: What educational testing really tells us*. Cambridge, MA: Harvard University Press.

Koretz, D. (2017). *The testing charade: Pretending to make schools better*. Chicago, IL: University of Chicago Press.

Madaus, G., Russell, M., & Higgins, J. (2009). *The paradoxes of high stakes testing: How they affect students, their parents, teachers, principals, schools, and society*. Charlotte, NC: Information Age.

Maylone, N. (2002). *The relationship of socioeconomic factors and district scores on the Michigan educational assessment program tests: An analysis.* (Unpublished doctoral dissertation). Eastern Michigan University, Ypsilanti, MI.

McMillan, J. H. (2004). *Classroom assessment: Principles and practice for effective instruction.* New York, NY: Pearson.

Messick, S. (1995). *Standards-based score interpretation: Establishing valid grounds for valid interpretations.* Proceedings on the joint conference of standard setting for large-scale assessments, Sponsored by the National Assessment Governing Board and the National Center for Educational Statistics. Washington, DC: Government Printing Office.

No Child Left Behind (NCLB), Act of 2001, Pub. L. No. 107-110, § 115, Stat. 1425 (January 8, 2002).

Sackey, A. N. L., Jr. (2014). *The influence of community demographics on student achievement on the Connecticut Mastery Test in mathematics and English language arts in Grade 3 through 8* (Unpublished doctoral dissertation). Seton Hall University, South Orange, NJ. Retrieved from http://scholarship.shu.edu/cgi/viewcontent.cgi?article=3033&context=dissertations.

Scherrer, J. (2014). The role of the intellectual in eliminating poverty: A response to Tierney. *Educational Researcher, 43,* 201–207.

Tanner, D. E. (2001). *Assessing academic achievement.* New York, NY: Allyn and Bacon.

Taylor, F. W. (1911). *Principles of scientific management.* New York, NY: Harper and Brothers.

Thompson, B. (2002). *Score reliability: Contemporary thinking on reliability issues.* New York, NY: Sage.

Tienken, C. H. (2017, July 5). Student test scores tell us more about the community they live in than what they know. *The Conversation.* Retrieved from https://theconversation.com/students-test-scores-tell-us-more-about-the-community-they-live-in-than-what-they-know-77934.

Tienken, C. H., Colella, A. J., Angelillo, C., Fox, M., McCahill, K., & Wolfe, A. (2017). Predicting middle school state standardized test results using family and community demographic data. *Research on Middle Level Education, 40*(1), 1-13.

United States Department of Education. (2009). *Race to the top: Executive summary.* Washington, DC: Author. Retrieved from https://www2.ed.gov/programs/racetothetop/executive-summary.pdf.

Wilkins, J. L. M. (1999). Demographic opportunities and school achievement. *Journal of Research in Education, 9*(1), 12–19.

Chapter 6

Adams, S. J., Heywood, J. S., & Rothstein, R. (2009). *Teachers, performance pay, and accountability: What education should learn from other sectors.* Washington, DC: Economic Policy Institute.

Au, W. (2011). Teaching under the new Taylorism: High-stakes testing and the standardization of the 21st century curriculum. *Journal of Curriculum Studies, 43*(1), 25-45. doi:10.1080/00220272.2010.521261

Bredo, E. (2002). The Darwinian center to the vision of William James. In J. Garrison, P. Poedeschi, & E. Bredo (Eds.), *William James and education.* New York, NY: Teachers College Press.

Brehm, J. W. (1972). *Response to loss of freedom: A theory of psychological reactance.* Morristown, NJ: General Learning Press.

Campbell, D. T. (1976). *Assessing the impact of planned social change.* Occasional paper series #8. Western Michigan University. Retrieved from http://citeseerx.ist.psu.edu/viewdoc/download?doi=10.1.1.170.6988&rep=rep1&type=pdf.

Campbell, D. T. (1979). Assessing the impact of planned social change. *Evaluation and Program Planning, 2*(1), 67–90.

Chistolini, S. (2009). *Teachers: Identity and ethics of the profession in Italy, United States of America, Poland, Belgium, Cyprus, Libya, Slovakia, Turkey.* Rome, Italy: Edizioni Kappa.

Dewey, J. (1924). The classroom teacher. *General Science Quarterly, 7,* 463-472.

Dewey, J. (1929). Sources of science in education. In E. R. Clapp (1952). *The use of resources in education.* Liveright: NY: Harper.

Doherty, K. M., & Jacobs, S. (2015). *State of the States 2015: Evaluating teaching, leading and learning.* Washington, DC: National Council on Teacher Quality. Retrieved from http://www.nctq.org/dmsStage/StateofStates2015.

Fryer, R. G. (2011). Teacher incentives and student achievement: Evidence from New York City public schools. *National Bureau of Economic Research.* Working paper 16850. Retrieved from http://www.nber.org/papers/w16850.

Glassman, M., Glassman, A., Champagne, P. J., & Zuegelder, M. T. (2010). Evaluating pay for performance systems: Critical issues for implementation. *Compensation & Benefits Review, 42*(4), 231-238.

Guis, M. (2012). The effects of teacher merit pay on academic attainment: An analysis using district-level data. *Journal of Economics and Economic Education Research, 13*(2), 93-108.

Herzberg, F. (1966). *Work and the nature of man.* Cleveland, OH: World Publishing.

Herzberg, F., Mausner, B., & Snyderman, B. B. (1959). *The motivation to work* (2nd ed.). New York, NY: John Wiley & Sons.

Kirp, D. (May 7, 2013). Failing the test. *Slate.* Retrieved from http://www.slate.com/articles/news_and_politics/science/2013/05/cheating_scandals_and_parent_rebellions_high_stakes_school_testing_is_doomed.html.

Koretz, D. (2009). *Measuring up: What educational testing really tells us.* Cambridge, MA: Harvard University Press.

Marsh, J. (2012). The micropolitics of implementing a school-based bonus policy: The case of New York City's compensation committees. *Educational Evaluation and Policy Analysis, 34*(2), 164-184.

McGregor, D. (1960). *The human side of enterprise.* New York, NY: McGraw Hill.

Mulder, M. (2014). Conceptions of professional competence. In S. Billett, C. Harteis, & H. Gruber (Eds.), *International handbook of research in profesional and practice-based earning* (pp. 107-137). Dordrecht: Springer.

Park, S., & Sturman, M. C. (2012). How and what you pay matters: The relative effectiveness of merit pay, bonuses, and long-term incentives on future job performance. *Compensation and Benefits Review, 44*(2), 80-85.

Porter, L. W., & Lawler, E. E. (1968). *Managerial attitudes and performance.* Homewood, IL: Dorsey Press and Richard D. Irwin.

Rescorla, R. A., & Wagner, A. R. (1972). A theory of Pavlovian conditioning: Variations in the effectiveness of reinforcement and nonreinforcement. In A. H. Black & W. F. Prokasy (Eds.), *Classical conditioning II* (pp. 64–99). New York, NY: Appleton-Century-Crofts.

Ryan, R. M., & Deci, E. L. (2000). Self-determination theory and the facilitation of intrinsic motivation, social development, and well-being. *American Psychologist, 55*, 68-78.

Shah, D. (2016). Transformational teamwork: The virtues and values of collaboration, Marshall. *Journal of Medicine, 2*(3).

Skinner, B. F. (1938). *The behavior of organisms: An experimental analysis.* New York, NY: Appleton-Century.

Skinner, B. F. (1953). *Science and human behavior.* New York: Simon and Schuster.

Springer, M. G., Ballou, D., Hamilton, L., Le, V., Lockwood, J. R., McCaffrey, D., Pepper, M., & Stecher, B. (2012). *Final report: Experimental evidence from the project on incentives in teaching.* Nashville, TN: National Center on Performance Incentives at Vanderbilt University.

Springer, M. G., Ballou, D., & Peng, X. (2008). *Impact of the Teacher Advancement Program on student test score gains: Findings from an independent appraisal.* Nashville, TN: National Center on Performance Incentives at Vanderbilt University.

Springer, M. G., Lewis, J. L., Podgursky, M. J., Ehlert, M. W., Taylor, L. L., Lopez, O. S., & Peng, A. (2009). *Governor's Educator Excellence Grant (GEEG) Program: Year three evaluation report.* Nashville, TN: National Center on Performance Incentives.

Springer, M. G., Pane, J. F., Le, V., McCaffrey, D. F., Burns, S. F., Hamilton, S., & Stecher, B. (2012). *Team pay for performance: Experimental evidence from the Round Rock Pilot project on team incentives.* Nashville, TN: National Center on Performance Incentives.

Stake, R. E. (1971). Testing hazards in performance contracting. *The Phi Delta Kappan, 52*(10), 583-589.

Tienken, C. H. (2009). Professional growth opportunities in the USA: What are important to teachers? In S. Chistolini (Ed.), *Teachers: Identity and ethics of the profession in Italy, United States of America, Poland, Belgium, Cyprus, Libya, Slovakia, Turkey* (pp. 17-34). Rome, Italy: Edizioni Kappa.

Tienken, C. H. (2016). Standardized test results can be predicted, so stop using them to drive education policymaking. In C. Tienken & C. Mullen (Eds.), *Education policy perils: Tackling the tough issues* (pp. 157-185). Philadelphia, PA: Taylor Francis Routledge.

Webb, R., Vulliamy, G., Hamalaninen, S., Sarja, A., Kimonen, E., & Nevalainen, R. (2004). A comparative analysis of primary teacher professionalism in England and Finland. *Comparative Education, 40*(1), 83-107.

Chapter 7

American Academy of Pediatrics. (2013). The crucial role of recess in school. *Pediatrics, 131*(1).

Black, D. S., Milam, J., & Sussman, S. (2009). Sitting-meditation interventions among youth: A review of treatment efficacy. *Pediatrics, 124*, 532-541. doi: 10.1542/peds.2008-3434

Carter, P. L., & Welner, K. G. (2013). *Closing the opportunity gap: What America must do to give every student a chance.* New York, NY: Oxford University Press.

Frank, J., Bose, B., & Schrobenhauser-Clonan, A. (2014). Effectiveness of a school-based yoga program on adolescent mental health, stress coping strategies, and attitudes toward violence: Findings from a high-risk sample. *Journal of Applied Psychology, 30*(1), 29-49.

Lee, J. (1915). *Play in education.* New York, NY: Macmillan.

Ratey, J. J. (2013). *Spark: The revolutionary new science of exercise and the brain.* New York, NY: Little, Brown, and Company.

Sahlberg, P. (2018). *FinnishED leadership: Four big, inexpensive ideas to transform education.* Thousand Oaks, CA: Corwin.

Scherrer, J. (2014). The role of the intellectual in eliminating poverty: A response to Tierney. *Educational Researcher, 43*, 201-207.

Serwacki, M., & Cook-Cottone, C. (2012). Yoga in the schools: A systematic review of the literature. *International Journal of Yoga Therapy, 101*(10).

Tienken, C. H. (2017). *Defying standardization: Creating curriculum for an uncertain future.* Lanham, MD: Rowman and Littlefield.

Waters, L., Barsky, A., Ridd, A., & Allen, K. (2015). Contemplative education: A systematic, evidence-based review of the effect of meditation interventions in schools. *Educational Psychology Review, 27*(1), 103-134.

Zhao, Y. (2018). *Reach for greatness: Personalizable education for all children.* Thousand Oaks, CA: Corwin.

Zylowska, L., Ackerman, D. L., Yang, M. H., Futrell, J. L., Horton, N. L., Hale, T. S., Pataki, C., & Smalley, S. L. (2008). Mindfulness meditation training in adults and adolescents with ADHD: A feasibility study. *Journal of Attention Disorders, 11*, 737-746.

Chapter 8

Achilles, C. M., & Reynolds, J. S., & Achilles, S. H. (1997). *Problem analysis: Responding to school complexity.* Larchmont, NY: Eye on Education

Bianchi, H., & Bell, R. (2008). The many levels of inquiry. *Science and Children, 46*(2), 26-29.

Dewey, J. (1910). *How we think*. Boston, MA: D.C. Heath & Co.

Dewey, J. (1916). *Democracy and education: An introduction to the philosophy of education*. New York, NY: Macmillan.

Dewey, J. (1929). *The sources of science of education*. New York, NY: Liveright.

Giles, H. H., McCutchen, S. P., & Zechiel, A. N. (1942). *Adventures in American education volume II: Exploring the curriculum*. New York, NY: Harper and Brothers.

Kuhlthau, C. C., Maniotes, K. K., & Caspari, A. K. (2015). *Guided inquiry: Learning in the 21st century*, 2nd ed. Santa Barbara, CA: Libraries Unlimited.

McDowell, M. (2017). *Rigorous PBL by design: Three shifts for developing confident and competent learners*. Thousand Oaks, CA: Corwin.

Mergendoller, J. R., Markham, T., Ravitz, J., & Larmer, J. (2006). Pervasive management of project based learning: Teachers as guides and facilitators. In C. Evertson, C. M. Weinstein, & C. S. Weinstein (Eds.), *Handbook of classroom management: Research, practice, and contemporary issues* (pp. 583-615). Mahwah, NJ: Erlbaum.

National Education Association of the United States, Committee of Ten on Secondary School Studies. (1893). *Report of the Committee of Ten on Secondary School Studies; with the Reports of the Conferences Arranged by the Committee*. New York, NY: National Education Association.

National Education Association of The United States Committee of Fifteen on Elementary Education. (1895). *Report of the Committee of Fifteen on Elementary Education, with the reports of the sub-committees*. New York, NY: National Education Association.

Salim, K., & Tiawa D. H. (2015). Implementation of structured inquiry based model learning toward students' understanding of geometry. *International Journal of Research in Education and Science (IJRES)*, *1*(1), 75-83.

Tienken, C. H. (2017). *Defying standardization: Creating curriculum for an uncertain future*. Lanham, MD: Rowman and Littlefield.

Chapter 9

Tienken, C. H., & Orlich, D. C. (2013). *The school reform landscape: Fraud, myth, and lies*. New York, NY: Rowman and Littlefield.

Index

Citizenship, community life and, 12
Code cracking
  application, 136
  merit pay and, 103–104
  rigor and, 70–71
  strategy of, 21–23, 34 (table)
Cognitive Rigor Matrix, 70, 71
Coleman, J. T., 81, 82
Collaboration, 31–32, 62
Commission on the Reorganization of
  Secondary Education, 42
Common Core State Standards (CCSS),
  56, 79
Compliance, creative. See Creative
  compliance
Confirmation Inquiry, 125
Constant-renewal, 45
Contemplative education. See
  Meditation
Cook-Cottone, C., 111
Creative compliance, 1–2, 19–36. See
  also specific strategies
  circumventing (strategy), 29–30,
    34 (table)
  code cracking (strategy), 21–23,
    34 (table)
  collaboration, 31–32
  compliance entrepreneur, 33
  creative insubordination, 19, 36
  creative leadership pathways,
    19–20
  failure as an option, 33–35
  flattery, 31
  Fountas and Pinnell reading
    scale, 22
  ingratiation (strategy), 30–31,
    34 (table)
  leadership take-away, 35
  merit pay and, 102–105
  negotiation (strategy), 26–27,
    34 (table)
  PBL and, 130–131
  practical framework, 50–51
  procrastination (strategy), 23–24,
    34 (table)
  recess of the mind and, 117–118
  rigor and, 69–71
  roots of, 19
  standardized test results and, 87–90
  strategies, 20–33

Student Growth Objectives, 21–23
  subordination, 20
  tacking (strategy), 25–26,
    34 (table)
  waivers (strategy), 28–29,
    34 (table)
Creative insubordination, 19, 36
Cremin, L. A., 4
Critique, ethics of, 11
Curriculum Paradigm, 3, 38, 39–40
  active participant and, 66
  progressivist philosophy of, 39
  useful characteristic of, 40

Darnell, B., 82
Deci, E. L., 98
Depth of Knowledge (DOK)
  framework, 70, 71
Desk reference critique questions (top
  10), 51–52 (table)
Dewey, J., 37, 38, 39, 40, 41, 45, 47, 48,
  58, 59, 62, 63, 65, 68, 85, 98, 100,
  106, 120, 121, 123, 125, 127, 128
Distributive justice, 14
Dochy, F., 46
Doherty, K. M., 75, 92

Ecological Systems Theory, 83
Education reform, defining of, 2, 8
Egalitarianism, 39
Ehlert, M. W., 95
Elementary and Secondary Education
  Act (ESEA), 56
Ely, R., 71
Engelhart, M. D., 71
ESSA. See Every Student Succeeds Act
Ethics, 8–18
  ambiguous rhetoric, 8–9
  beyond rhetoric, 9–10
  of caring, 13–14
  citizenship, community life and, 12
  of critique 11
  decision-making questions, 16
  distributive justice, 14
  education reform, defining of, 2, 8
  education reform, ethics within
    the context of, 10–14
  ethical dilemma, 15
  ethical responsibility, 15–16
  ethics leaders, types of, 11

CORWIN
A SAGE Publishing Company